Tony Chachere's

CAJUN COUNTRY COOKBOOK

Featuring
SEAFOOD
And
WILD GAME

Edited by
Griffin L. Gomez

Illustrations by
Aline Thistlethwaite

ISBN-09604580-1-8

ABOUT THE AUTHOR

Opelousas, Louisiana is in the heart of the Acadian (Cajun) country and is the one-time home of Jim Bowie, hero of the Alamo and inventor of the famed Bowie knife.

It is also the home of Tony Chachere, (Sash-er-ee), a noted sportsman, gourmet, businessman, raconteur, master salesman, chef and bon vivant of the area. He is of French descent and was born in Opelousas 85 years ago. Hard work followed by success has been the pattern of his life.

At age seven Tony was meeting the 2:30 a.m. train from New Orleans to pick up the big city morning papers for neighborhood delivery. Then he was off to school and back again for the afternoon papers after class was dismissed. At 12 he switched to delivering prescriptions and sundries for a local drug store. He soon graduated to "soda jerk," then clerk, and after intensive study and instruction, became a registered pharmacist and practiced this profession until he was 30. During two depression years he traveled as a drug salesman for a local wholesale drug firm, then founded his own wholesale drug business, working out of his garage at first, and finally parlaying a borrowed $100 into a million.

He retired at age fifty, but Tony is a man of action and after two years of leisure he began a new career as an insurance salesman with Equitable Life Insurance Society. He made the Millionaire's club his first year and every year thereafter. After 13 years he was installed in the Equitable Hall of Fame—the highest honor bestowed upon an agent.

In 1971 Tony retired for the second time. By 1972 he was only semi-retired, selling insurance occasionally, hunting, fishing and preparing his Cajun Country Cookbook.

For 40 years Tony has loved to cook, and his natural talent, his imagination and flair for always being the best, has earned him a reputation as a notable chef. Around Opelousas he is known as the

"Ole Master" of fine Cajun cuisine. His fishing and hunting camp on Bayou Big Alabama, in the Atchafalaya Swamp near Opelousas, is famous as a gourmet haven. His culinary talents have delighted palates from all over the United States, Mexico and Canada. For when good fellows get together Tony invariably heads for the kitchen while everyone else heads for dinner plates and the "chow line". His effervescent shout of "Tonight, I'm gonna make 'em cry!" is a promise of unsurpassed culinary delicacies soon to be conjured up.

Tony has fished or hunted practically every noteworthy lake, bayou and wood in Louisiana. He has fished Canadian and Mexican streams, hunted duck, deer and quail in Texas, white wing doves in Old Mexico, and pheasant and grouse in the Dakotas. Everywhere he's been he has enchanted native palates with his Cajun cooking, at times cooking for as many as 800 people. He's also picked up many good recipes along the way.

With his special knack, his famous Tony's Creole All-Purpose Seasoning, his new but already well-known Tony's Creole Roux, and his fabulous Tony's Creole BBQ Sauce ("You'll have to hide it from the children"), developed through the years, he's made them even better.

Since Tony's first book made its appearance, Tony has been a frequent guest on TV talk shows in Louisiana, Mississippi, Texas and as far East as Baltimore, Maryland. He has cooked for the governor of Louisiana, gave cooking demonstrations at the American School Food Association's national convention and features about him and his recipes have appeared in the food pages of numerous newspapers.

Tony is presently keeping busy by making personal appearances on TV and in department stores promoting his cookbook and his commercial products. "Tony Chachere's Cajun Country Cookbook", his first, is now in its 25th printing. His second book is his cookbook adapting Cajun cooking to the microwave oven. Another cookbook consists of Louisiana's Creole Seafood Recipes.

Tony says that with this book you can "make 'em cry!"

HUGH THISTLETHWAITE

TABLE OF CONTENTS

SEASONINGS, SAUCES, GRAVIES, DRESSINGS, MARINADES

So You Want to be a Good Cook 3
Tony's All-Purpose Famous Creole Seasoning 3
Basic Roux 4
How To Make a Brown Sauce or Gravy 4
Basic Vegetable Mixture 5
Basic Creole Dressing Mix 5
Basic Tomato Sauce 6
Tony's Creole Barbecue Sauce 6
How to Make a Cream Sauce 7
Basic Bread Stuffing 7
Baked Rice Dressing 8
Corn Bread Dressing 8
Lime Marinade 9
Sauce Marchand De Vin 9
Sauce Lalo Garcia 10
Madeira Sauce 10
Italian Meatless Mushroom Spaghetti Sauce 11
Steak Basting Sauce 11
Mushroom Steak Sauce 12
Barbecue Steak Sauce 12
Helen's Jezebell Sauce 13
All-Purpose Wild Game Marinade 13
Wild Game Sauce 13
Creole Seafood Cocktail Sauce 14
Sherry Sauce Lucille 14
Chinese Brown Sauce 14
Shrimp Remoulade Sauce 15
Yankee Gravy 15
Chinese Mustard Sauce 15
New Orleans Tartar Sauce 16
Wine Tartar Sauce 16
Garlic Sauce 16
Horseradish Sauce 17
Sour Cream Dressing 17
Tony's Hollandaise Sauce 17
Raisin Sauce for Baked Ham 18
How to Cook Rice 18

SALADS AND SALAD DRESSINGS

Opelousas French Dressing 21
Creole Salad Dressing 21
Mayonnaise 21
Roquefort Dressing 22
The Cajun Way to Add Garlic to a Salad 22
Madge's Spinach Salad 22
Green Bean Salad 22
Crab Meat Salad 23
Shrimp Salad 23
Party Shrimp Mold 24
Tomato Shrimp Salad 24
Stuffed Avocado Salad 24
Tomato Aspic 25
Cherry Gelatin Salad 25
Chicken Salad 25
Lime Gelatin Salad 26
Harold's Hand Salad 26

GUMBOS AND SOUPS

Gumbo 29
File 29
Crawfish Gumbo 30
Tony's Oyster Chowder 30
Shrimp and Okra Gumbo 31
Seafood Gumbo 31
Guinea Gumbo 32
Chicken and Okra Gumbo 33
Creole Bouillon (Soup) 33
Creole Vegetable Soup 34
Delicious Corn Soup 34
Cucumber Soup 35
Tony's Pinto Beans and Smoked Ham Hocks 36
Tony's Leek Soup 36
Tony's Cas-Ca-Ra 37
Black Bean Soup 37
Turtle Soup 38

SEAFOOD

Tony's Crawfish Casserole 40
Tony's Crab Soup 40
Tony's Crawfish Cocktail 41
Tony's Crawfish Boulets and Stuffed Shells 41
Tony's Crawfish Bisque 42
Tony's Fried Crawfish Tails 42
Tony's Crawfish Etouffee 43
Tony's Crawfish Stew Emile 43
Crawfish Crepes 44
Tony's Crawfish Pie 44
Tony's Crawfish Egg Rolls 45
Heavenly Eggs Crawfish 46
Guidry's Fried Stuffed Hard Shell Crabs 46
Tony's Secret to Cooking Live Crawfish, Shrimp & Crab 47
Fried Soft Shell Crabs 47
Boiled Crabs in a Chest 48
Broiled Soft Shell Crabs 48
Stuffed Crab Shells 48
Opelousas Barbecued Crabs 49
Crab Meat and Green Peppers 49
Opelousas Oyster Loaf 50
Oysters Poulette 50
Oysters Rockefeller 51
Oysters en Brochette 51
Oysters Bienville 52
Oyster Stew 52
Huitres au Diable 53
Frog Man 53
Fried Frogs 54
Frog Legs with Tartar Sauce 54
Frog Legs a la Sauce Piquante 55
Tony's Broiled Louisiana Frogs 55
Frog Legs Provencal 56
Turtle Stew 56
McJunkins Turtle Sauce Piquante 57
Claude's Turtle on the Bayou 57
Black Pepper Shrimp 58
Broiled Shrimp a la Tony 58
Shrimp and Eggplant Jambalaya 58
Shrimp Chinese Style 59
Chinese Skillet Shrimp 59
Shrimp Fried Rice 60
Shrimp Kee Kee 60
Pat Huval's (Henderson, LA) Fried Shrimp 61
Smoked Fish 61
Six Ways To Fry Fish 62
Baked Red Snapper 62
Mushroom-Stuffed Baked Red Snapper 63
Pompano en Papillote 64
Flounder with Sauterne Sauce 64
Stuffed Flounder 65
Walleyed Perch 65
Filet of Sole Marguery 66
Trout Marguery 66
Tony's Trout Meuniere 67
Tony's Fish Courtbouillon 67
Tony's Boiled Fish with Bienville Sauce 68
Barbecued Fish 68
Tony's Fish Swazela 69
Fish Croquettes 69
Sherry Ketchup Baked Fish 70
Jim's Choupique, Bayou Courtableau Style 70
Tony's Blackened Redfish 71
Jim Bowie's Creole Garfish Boulets 71
Raw Fish Seviche 71
Tony's Crawfish Supreme 72

GAME

Tony's Alligator Sauce Piquante 74
Brice Palmer's Fried Alligator 74
Tony's Barbecued Alligator Tail 75
Roast Goose with Sauerkraut & Bread Dumpling . 75
Jim Bowie's Clay Baked Duck 76
Coot in Soy Sauce 76
Wild Ducks a la George Broussard 77
Baked Teal with Oysters 78
Mexican Fried Dove 78
Sherried Doves 79
Smothered Doves Acadienne 79
Dove Casserole 80
Tony's Quail Recipe 80
Quail en Casserole 81
Mexican Baked Quail 81
Quail Sauteed in Wild Game Sauce 81
Creamed Snipe 82
Broiled Brandied Snipe 82
Smothered Snipe 82
Grouse in White Wine 84
Grouse with Orange Slices 84
Roast Grouse with Wine Sauce 85
Roast Pheasant with Cream and Brandy 85
Louisiana Cajun's Squirrel Stew 86
Baked Juicy Swamp Rabbit 87
Roast Rabbit 87
Roast Venison 88
Tasty Venison Chops 88
Breaded Venison Schnitzel 89
Venison Parmesan 89
Venison Daube Glace 90
Creamed Venison Chops 91
Baked Coon and Sweet Potatoes 91
Cleve's Smothered Armadilo 92
Tony's Nutria Sauce Piquante 93

MEATS AND POULTRY

Tony's Chicken and Sausage Jambalaya 72
Charcoal Ribeye Steak 97
Creole Baked Tongue 97
Marinated Pork Grillades 98
Creole Salt Pork 98
Barbecued Pork Ribs w/ Special Chinese Sauce 98
Pork Backbone Stew 99
Chinese Pork Chops 99
Veal Oscar 100
Tony's Baked Picnic Ham 101
Johnson's Boudin Blanc 101
Creole Hogshead Cheese 102
Creole Smoked Pork Sausage 102
Isabell's Country Style Creole Roast Pork 103
Grilled Spareribs 103
Savory Lamb Chops 104
Lamb Stew with Olives 104
Lamb Chops in Wine Sauce 105
Lamb Fries 105
Creole Smothered Liver 105
Baked Liver and Onions 106
Italian Rollettes 106
Italian Pizza 107
Chili Con Carne 107
Tony's He-Man Chili 108
Hot Tamale Pie 108
Tony's Meat Balls and Spaghetti 109
Sweetbreads en Brouchette 110
Tripe Creole 110
Creamed Sweetbreads with Mushrooms 111
Creole Style Sweetbreads 111
Stuffed Ponce Bourree 112
Opelousas Baked Long Island Duck 112
Opelousas Baked Chicken 113
Tony's Old Fashioned Chicken Stew 113
Tony's Breaded Fried Chicken 114
Tony's Crispy Fried Chicken 114
Tony's Chicken Saute Aux Gros Onions & Olives 115
Broiled Chicken Livers with Bacon and Water Chestnuts 115
Paella 116
Japanese Chicken-Pork Barbecue 116
Dee's Chicken and Spaghetti 117
Pigeonneaux en Paradis 117
Tony's Roast Turkey 118
Casserole of Guinea Hen with Brandy Sauce 119
Tony's Baked Cornish Game Hens 120
Cornish Hens with Basting Sauce 121
Chachere's Deep Fried Turkey 121

Vegetables and Casseroles

Louisiana Yam, Coconut & Orange Casserole 125
Spiced, Baked Louisiana Yams 125
French-Fried Sweet Potatoes 126
Yummy Louisiana Produce Bake 126
Yam Holiday Party Candle Cakes 127
Orange Candied Sweet Potatoes 127
Baked Golden Louisiana Yams 128
Cabbage and Fresh Pork Sausage 128
Tony's Cabbage Casserole 128
Stuffed Cabbage Rolls 129
Escalloped Cabbage 129
Fried Eggplant Casserole 130
Stuffed Eggplant 130
Fried Eggplants 131
Eggplant with Shrimp Casserole 131
Eggplant, Crabmeat Casserole 132
Seafood Casserole 132
Tony's Crabmeat Casserole 133
Fried Okra 133
Maquechou 134
Fried Green Tomatoes 134
Tony's Meat and Spaghetti Casserole 135
Tomato and Bacon Casserole 135
Pork and Bean Casserole 135
Baked Stuffed Tomatoes 136
Smothered Okra and Tomatoes 136
Broccoli Casserole 137
Turnip Casserole 137
Marinated Green Bell Peppers 137
Tony's Crawfish Stuffed Bell Peppers 138
Stuffed Green Bell Peppers 138
Tony's Creamed Garlic Spinach 139
Spinach Casserole Lucille 139
Chicken Artichoke Casserole 140
Asparagus Cream Sauce Casserole 140
Tuna Fish Cauliflower Casserole 141
Casserole of String Beans and Carrots Au Gratin 141
Stewed Corn 142
Creamed Onions 142
French Fried Onions 142
Smothered Creole Leeks 143
Cheese and Onion Pie 143
Brabant Potatoes 143
Irish Potato Casserole 144
Johnny Mazette 144
Squash Casserole 145
Zucchini Squash with Dill Sauce 145
Cucumbers Stuffed with Ham and Sour Pickles 146
Stuffed Cooked Cucumbers 147
New Orleans Red Beans and Rice 147

EGGS GRITS PANCAKES

How to Fry an Egg ... 151
Another Way to Cook Eggs ... 151
Heavenly Eggs ... 151
Scrambled Eggs with Green Peppers ... 151
Ham and Eggs Jambalaya ... 152
Eggs Florentine ... 152
Eggs Benedict ... 152
Frank's Spanish Omelet ... 153
Tony's Crabmeat Omelette ... 153
Shirred Eggs ... 154
Tony's Heavenly Pancakes ... 154
Corn Meal Batter Cakes ... 155
Potato Pancakes ... 155
Creole Garlic Grits for Breakfast ... 155
Jim Bowie's Hush Puppies ... 156
Jim Bowie's Couche — Couche et Caille ... 156

BREADS

Tony's Hot Tamales ... 158
Hard Crust French Bread ... 159
Homemade Bread ... 159
Dilly Casserole Bread ... 160
Grated Yam Bread ... 160
Garlic Bread ... 161
Jim Bowie Hoecakes ... 161
Pain Perdu ... 161
Golden Snack Bread ... 162
Aunt Lulu's Grit Bread ... 162
Hot Mexican Cornbread ... 163
Spoon Bread ... 163
Bread Dumplings ... 164
Beer Muffins ... 164
Tony's Ole-Fashioned Creole Corn Bread ... 165
Tony's Biscuits ... 165
Roughneck Hot Rolls ... 166
Popover ... 166
Jeannine's Pumpkin Muffins ... 166

SWEETS

Offshore Pie Dough ... 168
Coconut Roustabout Cookies ... 168
Buttermilk Pie ... 169
Opelousas Pralines ... 169
Creole Benne Pralines ... 169
Creamy Smooth Pecan Pralines ... 170
Pecan Pie ... 170
Ritz Pie ... 170
Date Torte ... 171
Cherries Jubilee ... 171
French Chocolate Cup ... 171
Baked Alaska ... 172
Meringue Shells ... 173
Sugared Pecans ... 173
Brownies ... 174
Date Cake ... 174
Yankee-Rebel Feud Cake ... 175
Apple Cake St. Amand ... 175
"Sock It To Me" Cake ... 176
Aunt Happy's Cake ... 176
Date Balls ... 177
Whiskey Balls ... 177
Brandy Balls ... 177
Molasses Popcorn Balls ... 177
Lizzie's Cookies ... 178
Party Cookies ... 178
Peach Flambeau ... 178
Banana Nut Bread ... 179
Creole Style Homemade Peach Ice Cream ... 179
Tony's Creole Custard Flan ... 180
Creole Pecan Custard ... 180
Patsy's Blackberry Cobbler ... 181
Tony's Crepe Suzettes ... 181
Louisiana Rice Pudding ... 182
Kiddy Peanut Butter Candy Wheels ... 182
Holiday Treat ... 182
Les Oreiles de Cochon ... 183
Bread Pudding with Whiskey Sauce ... 183

Beverages, Hors d'Oeuvres, Delicacies

Russell Green's Rolled Alligator Roast ... 186
Garbo's Caponata ... 186
Creole Dripped Coffee ... 187
Irish Coffee ... 187
Cafe Diable ... 187
Wild Cherry Bounce ... 188
Blackberry Wine ... 188
Creole Egg Nog ... 188
Bull Shot ... 189
Sazerac Cocktail ... 189
Ramos Gin Fizz ... 189
Cream de Menthe Frappe ... 190
Golden Champagne Punch ... 190
Brandy Fruit Champagne ... 190
Jalapeno Pepper Hors d' Oeuvres ... 191
Hot Pepper Jelly ... 191
Pink Pickled Eggs ... 191
Big Alabama Bayou Roasted Pecans & Hot Buttered Rum ... 192
Shrimp Canapes ... 192
Crackers Deluxe ... 192
Pickled Okra ... 193
Tomato Pickles ... 193
Shrimp Hors d'Oeuvres ... 194
Creamy Nutty Tuna Sandwiches ... 194
Ham Balls ... 194
Swedish Meat Balls ... 195
Veal Scallopini Dip ... 195
Cucumber-Chicken Spread ... 196
Deviled Ham Dip ... 196
Stuffed Celery ... 196

TONY CHACHERE'S INSTANT CREOLE ROUX AND GRAVY MIX

For Gumbos and Stews
Fry seasoned meat in small amount of oil or margarine. When brown, add chopped vegetables and saute for 5 or 10 minutes. Mix two tablespoons Creole Roux to each pint of cold liquid. Let it come to a boil, lower heat and simmer until tender. Add more or less roux to thicken or thin. For seafoods use same procedure, except add seafood last and cook for 30 minutes.

Delicious Cajun Gravy
Mix two tablespoons Tony's Roux in one cup cold water. Add tablespoon sherry wine and one tablespoon each chopped onion tops and parsley. In a small sauce pan, cook over medium heat, stirring while gravy comes to a boil. Lower heat and cook for one minute. Serve over mashed potatoes, noodles, rice, hot meat sandwich, etc.

Creole Brown Sauce
Melt two tablespoons butter or margarine in a small sauce pan. Add two tablespoons Tony's Creole Roux and Gravy Mix, stirring constantly while adding one cup cold milk or cream. Blend well, let come to a boil, lower heat and cook for one minute.

You can use mushrooms, cheese, wine, cucumber dills, horseradish, fish stock, or what-have-you to improve this sauce.

Packed one dozen 10 ounce sifter top containers to case. $21.00 per case shipped prepaid. (No broken cases.)

SEASONINGS
SAUCES
GRAVIES
DRESSINGS
MARINADES

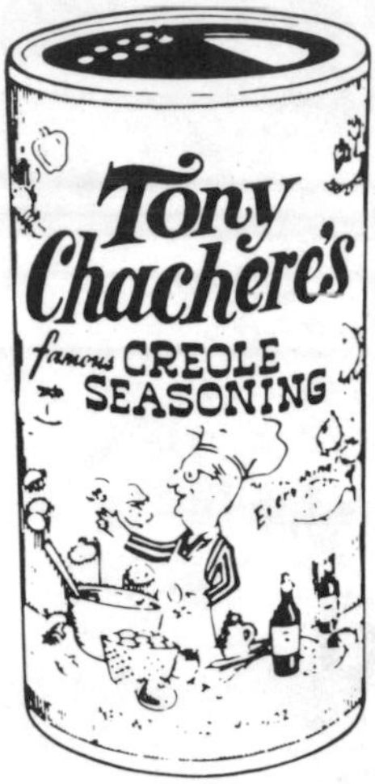

TONY CHACHERE'S FAMOUS CREOLE SEASONING

Tony's Famous Creole Seasoning is an exact blend of the very spices most prized by Creole cooks. It goes perfectly with all meats, seafood, poultry, vegetables, eggs, soups, stews and salads and for **barbecue and French fries, there is no finer seasoning. Use it anytime anywhere on any type of food.**

DIRECTIONS

Use it like salt. When it's salty enough, it's seasoned to perfection. Use at the rate of one heaping tablespoonful to a three pound fryer, or three pound roast. For delicious barbecue season all over and then refrigerate for at least one hour before cooking.

Imitated but never Duplicated
50 Years of Experience proves that!

If you can't find Tony Chachere's Famous Creole Seasoning, do the best you can with salt and pepper, or you can call us at our Toll Free Number—

CALL OUR TOLL FREE NUMBER
1-800-551-9066

Remember the Secret of all Good Cooking is in the Seasoning.

SO YOU WANT TO BE A GOOD COOK!

With Tony Chachere's CAJUN COUNTRY COOKBOOK you can be the best cook in your crowd — male or female. If you already are, we guarantee that within these pages you'll find many "Cajun s'yle" dishes that will surprise and delight the most discriminating of your friends. It's easy! To use most of these recipes all you need to know are a few basics:

1. How to make a roux. (pronounced rue)
2. How to make a brown sauce or gravy.
3. How to make a cream sauce.
4. How to get the right vegetable mixture.
5. How to make a tomato sauce.
6. How to season with spices and herbs.

Number 6 is easy. How to season? Simply substitute with Tony's Creole Seasoning and use like salt.

TONY'S ALL-PURPOSE FAMOUS CREOLE SEASONING

The secret of good cooking is in the seasoning. After 40 years of cooking and blending, Tony has come up with this tried and tested mixture of spices, herbs and seasoning. These are so well blended that you use Tony's Creole Seasoning as you would salt. The quantity below is good for many delicious meals. Store in an airtight jar.

THIS RECIPE IS WORTH THE PRICE OF THE BOOK

26-ounce box free flowing salt (Morton's)
1½-ounce box ground black pepper
2-ounce bottle ground red pepper
1-ounce bottle pure garlic powder
1-ounce bottle chili powder

Mix well and use like salt. When it's salty enough, it's seasoned to perfection. Use generously on everything except when the recipes in this book call for something else. If too peppery for children, add more salt to mixture, then season to taste.

TO SEASON SEAFOOD — use half of above mixture and add:

1 teaspoon powdered thyme
1 teaspoon bay leaf
1 teaspoon sweet basil

BASIC ROUX

The basis for all stews and gumbos

1 cup flour (all-purpose)
1 cup cooking oil, your favorite brand (I use margarine)

Heat oil in heavy pot or Dutch oven. When oil is hot, gradually add flour, stirring continuously until well mixed. Lower flame and continue stirring until chocolate brown. When roux is chocolate brown, remove from pot and set aside. If roux remains in the pot it will continue to cook and get too dark.

Always use warm water to dissolve the roux.

While you're at it, make more than enough as it keeps well in or out of the refrigerator.

HOW TO MAKE A BROWN SAUCE OR GRAVY

(For all meats and game)

Pan drippings
1 tablespoon chopped green scallions (onion tops)
1 tablespoon parsley, minced
Flour (enough to thicken)

Use pan drippings (remove excess fat) of meat or game. To this add scallions, parsley and enough flour and water to the mixture to thicken. Cook about 5 minutes.

If desired add mushrooms and if you like gravy on the sweet side, add 1 tablespoon currant jelly.

BASIC VEGETABLE MIXTURE

1 onion
½ green bell pepper
2 sticks celery
1 clove garlic

Run vegetables through meat grinder or blender. (Makes 1 cup). You can double this recipe to suit your needs.

A Cajun would die if you took his garlic and onions away.

BASIC CREOLE DRESSING MIX

(For wild game and fowl)
½ pound lean pork
½ pound lean beef
1 pound gizzards
2 sticks margarine
2 large onions, chopped fine
4 sticks celery chopped fine
2 cloves garlic, chopped fine
1 can chicken bouillon
1 tablespoon Worcestershire sauce
Tony's Creole Seasoning or salt and pepper to taste

Run meat through grinder. Melt 1 stick margarine in a Dutch oven and fry meat until brown, about 20 minutes. Add onions, celery and garlic, stir and cook until soft. Add Worcestershire sauce, bouillon and 1 stick margarine. Stir well, bring to a boil and simmer for about 2 hours. Season to taste with Tony's Creole Seasoning or salt and pepper. (Serves 12)

NOTE: To the above mixture you can add —
(1) For RICE DRESSING (a Cajun calls it "Dirty Rice"): About 6 cups of boiled rice. Wilt ½ cup chopped green onion tops (scallions) and ½ cup minced parsley in ¼ stick melted margarine. Mix well with rice.

(2) For CORNBREAD DRESSING: 6 cups crumbled corn bread combined with green mixture as in No. 1.

(3) For BREAD DRESSING: 6 cups croutons (or bread crumbs) and same proportion green seasoning as in No. 1.

BASIC TOMATO SAUCE

1 stick margarine
1 6-ounce can tomato sauce
½ teaspoon sugar
1 teaspoon Worcestershire sauce
1 teaspoon lemon juice
Tony's Creole Seasoning or salt and pepper
2 cups Basic Vegetables (See page 5) (run through meat grinder)
1 quart water

Melt margarine in heavy saucepan, add tomato sauce, sugar and cook 5 minutes. Add all other ingredients plus 1 quart water. Simmer for 2 hours over low heat until thick. Add more water if needed and season to taste. (Makes about 4 cups)

FOR ITALIAN DISHES: add to above different herbs, cheese, etc.

FOR FISH DISHES: add mushrooms, shrimp, crab meat, etc., to above.

TONY'S CREOLE BARBECUE SAUCE

1 quart Wesson oil
1 whole pod garlic
6 sticks celery
2 pounds onions
5 green bell peppers
1 pint water
Salt and pepper to taste

Chop all vegetables. Cook the above for at least 2 hours and then add balance of ingredients:

1 pound margarine
6-ounce jar yellow mustard
14-ounce bottle Heinz chili sauce
Juice of 1 lemon
2 tablespoons Worcestershire
3-ounce bottle Louisiana Red Hot Sauce
1 quart water

Cook until well mixed and well blended. Use the oil on top for basting and serve the cooked vegetables as a side dish.

So good you can eat it on bread!

Of course I sell this in 18-oz. bottles! See the back of book.

HOW to MAKE a CREAM SAUCE

1 pint hot coffee cream
½ stick margarine
2 teaspoons flour

Melt butter in a saucepan over medium heat. Add flour, stir well, and add coffee cream (slowly) while stirring. Continue stirring until you get a thick sauce.

To this sauce can be added mushrooms, shrimp, crab meat, grated cheese, white wine, lemon juice, egg yolks, etc. or any of these. (Makes 2 cups)

BASIC BREAD STUFFING

8 cups bread crumbs or cubes
½ cup butter
1 cup chopped onions
1 cup diced celery with leaves
½ teaspoon Tabasco sauce
½ teaspoon poultry seasoning
2 tablespoons chopped parsley
¼ cup chicken bouillon
1½ teaspoon salt

Melt the butter, add onions, celery, Tabasco, poultry seasoning and salt. Cook until onions are tender, but not brown. Combine with bread crumbs and parsley. Add bouillon, toss lightly with a fork until well mixed. This amount is enough for a 12-pound turkey or two 6-pound chickens. Use ¾ cup stuffing per pound of dressed weight.

If desired, stuffing may be baked separately and served with chicken, veal or beef. Place stuffing in foil, seal edges tightly, and bake in moderate oven, 350 to 375 degrees, for 35 minutes; or in slow oven (325 degrees) for 45 minutes.

For MUSHROOM STUFFING: add ½ cup canned sliced mushrooms to basic recipe and omit bouillon.

For RICE STUFFING: substitute 3 cups cooked rice and 5 cups bread in basic recipe.

CORNBREAD STUFFING: substitute 4 cups cornbread crumbs and 4 cups bread crumbs for bread in basic recipe.

OYSTER STUFFING: add 1 pint oysters, drained and coarsely chopped, to basic recipe.

BAKED RICE DRESSING
(Dirty Rice for you fellow Cajuns)

- ½ pound ground lean pork
- ½ cup ground chicken gizzards
- 1 cup raw rice
- 1 can onion soup
- 1 can cream of mushroom soup
- 1 cup chopped green onion tops (scallions)
- ⅓ cup celery chopped fine
- 1 cup parsley, minced
- ⅓ cup finely chopped onions
- ⅓ cup chopped green bell pepper
- Red and black pepper to taste

Mix ground meat with the raw rice. Add onion, bell pepper, celery, onion tops and parsley. Mix in the soups and season with red and black pepper. Put into a heavy casserole dish and cover with close-fitting cover in order to retain all the juice. Bake at 325 degrees for 2 hours. (Serves 4)

CORN BREAD DRESSING
(Tony's Special)

- 1 pound chicken gizzards
- 1 pound lean ground meat (½ pork and ½ beef)
- 2 sticks margarine
- 4 chopped onions
- 4 sticks chopped celery
- 2 cloves minced garlic
- 1 tablespoon Worcestershire sauce
- 2 10-ounce cans chicken bouillon
- 4 cups corn bread
- ½ cup chopped green onion tops
- Tony's Creole Seasoning or salt and pepper

In a Dutch oven, fry meat in margarine until brown. Add onions, celery and garlic. Saute five minutes, add bouillon soup, Worcestershire, season to taste. Bring to boil and simmer for 2 hours. Mix in 4 cups corn bread and ½ cup onion tops. Bring seasoning up to taste. (Makes 10 servings)

LIME MARINADE
For Ribs

3 to 4 pound strip of spareribs
¾ cup lime juice
½ cup salad oil
3 tablespoons brown sugar
½ teaspoon coriander
½ teaspoon ginger
½ teaspoon salt
1 lime cut in wedges

Combine all ingredients. Place spareribs in shallow baking dish and cover with mixture. Cover and refrigerate overnight or 4 to 6 hours. Drain and reserve marinade. Place spareribs, rib side up, on rack in a roasting pan and cover tightly. Bake at 350 degrees for 1 hour. Uncover, turn over and brush with reserve marinade. Continue to bake for 1½ hours brushing with reserve marinade every 30 minutes. Remove from oven and serve on heated platter. Garnish with lime wedges. (Makes 4 servings)

SAUCE MARCHAND DE VIN

1 stick butter
½ cup chopped mushrooms
⅓ cup chopped green onion tops
6 pods chopped garlic
½ cup minced ham
2 tablespoons flour
Tony's Creole Seasoning to taste
1 cup beef bouillon
1 cup Burgundy wine

Melt butter, saute mushrooms, ham, onion tops, onions and garlic. Add flour and seasoning. Brown well. Blend in bouillon and wine. Simmer over low heat 1 hour. Makes 2 cups. Serve on unseasoned charcoal broiled steaks.

SAUCE LALO GARCIA

A hot sauce for doves, quail or any wild game.

1 onion, chopped
1 green bell pepper chopped
2 sticks celery, chopped
1 whole tomato, diced
6 long, green Louisiana red hot peppers, chopped (Jalapeños may be substituted)
1 stick margarine

Saute all vegetables in melted margarine for about 10 minutes.

MADEIRA SAUCE

(Meat Sauce)

1/3 cup Madeira wine
2 tablespoons butter
2 tablespoons flour
2 cups beef bouillon
Salt and freshly ground black pepper

Melt butter over low heat, add flour and stir until smooth. Add bouillon and cook until thick, stirring until smooth. Stir in Madeira, salt, pepper and simmer for 5 minutes. Makes about 2 cups. Ideal for meats.

ITALIAN MEATLESS MUSHROOM SPAGHETTI SAUCE

A good thick sauce, delicious over any pasta, not only spaghetti, and is a basis for a tempting fish variation.

¼ cup olive oil
¼ cup chopped onions
¼ cup chopped celery
½ cup sliced mushrooms, fresh or canned
6-ounce can tomato paste
2 cups hot water
2 tablespoons chopped parsley
1 teaspoon salt
½ teaspoon oregano
Dash of pepper
1 leaf sweet basil
½ pound spaghetti, cooked and drained
Grated Parmesan cheese

Cook onions, celery and mushrooms in olive oil until lightly brown. Mix tomato paste, water and seasoning. Add to vegetables. Simmer 30 to 40 minutes. (Serves 4)

STEAK BASTING SAUCE

¾ cup olive oil
¾ cup dry red wine
1 tablespoon lime juice
1 garlic clove, mashed
⅓ cup finely chopped onions
1 teaspoon oregano
½ teaspoon thyme
1 teaspoon sugar
1 teaspoon salt
Freshly ground black pepper

Combine ingredients and beat or shake until well blended. Spread liberally over steak while cooking, both before and after turning.

Throughout this book you will find the use of onion tops. Most people call them scallions. They are one and the same.

MUSHROOM STEAK SAUCE

¼ pound fresh mushrooms or 1 4-ounce can sliced mushrooms
3 tablespoons butter
1 medium onion, finely chopped
1 clove garlic, minced
1 10½-ounce can beef bouillon
1½ tablespoons tomato paste
⅛ teaspoon ground black pepper
2 teaspoons cornstarch
1 teaspoon cold water
2 tablespoons Madeira wine

Rinse, pat dry and slice fresh mushrooms, making about 1¼ cups, or drain canned mushrooms. Set aside. In small saucepan heat 1 tablespoon butter, add onion and garlic, saute until brown. Add bouillon, tomato paste and black pepper, bring to a boil. Reduce heat, cover and simmer 10 minutes.

Meanwhile, in a small skillet, heat remaining 2 tablespoons butter, add mushrooms, saute until brown, set aside. Blend cornstarch with water, mix some of the hot onion mixture into cornstarch mixture and return to saucepan.

Cook, stirring constantly, until clear and thickened. Add sauteed mushrooms and wine. Bring to boiling point and serve over steak, meatloaf, etc. (Makes about 2 cups)

BARBECUE STEAK SAUCE

2 sticks butter or margarine
¼ cup lemon juice
¼ cup Worcestershire

Melt butter, add lemon juice and Worcestershire sauce. Baste meat with this sauce. Pour over barbecued meat.

HELEN'S JEZEBELL SAUCE

10-ounce jar pineapple preserves
10-ounce jar apple jelly
6-ounce jar horseradish (from the dairy case)
½ can dry mustard, 1½-ounce size
1 teaspoon ground black pepper

Mix all ingredients together, let set in refrigerator 1 hour. Serve on sliced ham, meats, etc.

ALL-PURPOSE WILD GAME MARINADE

1 cup water
2 tablespoons vinegar
1 sliced lemon
½ dozen crushed peppercorns
2 to 3 carrot slices
1 stick green celery, chopped
1 teaspoon bay leaf
2 or 3 sprigs parsley
2 or 3 crushed whole cloves
1 tablespoon Tony's Creole Seasoning
2 cloves garlic
1 onion, chopped fine
2 tablespoons oil

Marinate overnight for all wild game, the longer the better.

WILD GAME SAUCE

1 cup seedless white grapes
4 tablespoons butter
½ cup port wine
⅛ teaspoon ground cloves
2 tablespoons mushrooms, finely chopped
½ cup pecans, finely chopped

In a saucepan put grapes and 1 cup water. Bring to a boil, cover. Reduce heat and simmer for 5 minutes. Drain off water, add butter, wine and cloves. Cover and simmer for 5 minutes. Stir in mushrooms and simmer for 5 minutes. Add pecans and serve over game immediately. (Makes about 2½ cups)

CREOLE SEAFOOD COCKTAIL SAUCE

(For oysters, shrimp, crawfish, etc.)

1 cup catsup
1 tablespoon horseradish
1 teaspoon Worcestershire sauce
Salt to taste
1 teaspoon Louisiana Red Hot Sauce
½ cup celery, chopped very fine

Mix all ingredients, then mix with oysters. Serve with crackers. We also sell a premixed version - see back of book.

SHERRY SAUCE LUCILLE

1 cup mayonnaise
½ cup Heinz chili sauce
3 tablespoons sherry wine
½ teaspoon Worcestershire sauce
Salt and pepper to taste

Combine all ingredients and chill thoroughly before serving. Excellent as a dressing for crabs, shrimp or lobsters. (Makes about 1½ cups)

CHINESE BROWN SAUCE

2 tablespoons cornstarch
3 cups chicken bouillon
2 tablespoons soy sauce
½ teaspoon sugar
Freshly ground black pepper

Mix cornstarch with ½ cup cold bouillon. Combine with remaining bouillon, soy sauce, sugar and pepper. Bring to a boil, reduce heat and simmer until thickened, stirring occasionally. Serve hot. (Makes about 3 cups.)

SHRIMP REMOULADE SAUCE

10 ounces olive oil
5 ounces vinegar
7½ ounces Dijon mustard or Creole mustard
5 ounces tomato catsup
5 tablespoons fresh horseradish (from dairy case)
5 cloves garlic
1 teaspoon Tabasco sauce
Salt to taste

Blend ingredients as listed. Serve over boiled shrimp. Mix with shredded lettuce and finely sliced celery. (Enough for 10 servings)

YANKEE GRAVY

1 cup milk
1½ teaspoons flour
2 teaspoons chicken fat (pan drippings)
¼ teaspoon salt

Melt fat and remove from heat. Add flour, stir until smooth. Return to heat. Add cold liquid all at once and cook, stirring constantly until thick. Cook over direct heat 5 minutes, stirring occasionally. Add salt.

If you like it sweet, add sugar to taste.

CHINESE MUSTARD SAUCE

¼ cup boiling water
¼ cup dry mustard
½ teaspoon salt
2 teaspoons salad oil

Stir boiling water into dry mustard. Add salt and salad oil. Serve on egg roll, fried shrimp, etc.

NEW ORLEANS TARTAR SAUCE

1 cup mayonnaise (freshly made with olive oil)
1 teaspoon powdered mustard
1 teaspoon onion, grated
2 tablespoons parsley, minced
½ clove garlic, put through press
⅛ teaspoon red pepper
2 tablespoons chopped dill pickle
2 tablespoons capers, drained and chopped
1 tablespoon minced green onion tops

Combine all ingredients, mix well, and serve with fillet of trout and other seafood.

WINE TARTAR SAUCE

1 cup mayonnaise
¼ cup sherry
3 tablespoons drained sweet pickles, relish or chopped sweet pickles
2 tablespoons minced parsley
2 tablespoons chopped pimento-stuffed olives
1 teaspoon chopped capers
1 tablespoon minced onions
Dash Tabasco sauce
Salt to taste

Mix all ingredients together well. Makes about 1½ cups sauce. Good with any broiled or fried fish.

GARLIC SAUCE

1 stick butter
5 tablespoons lemon juice
1 teaspoon chopped garlic

Brown the butter and add lemon juice and garlic. Season to taste.

HORSERADISH SAUCE

2 tablespoons prepared horseradish
1 tablespoon tarragon vinegar
1 teaspoon prepared mustard
½ pint cream
1 teaspoon minced onions
¼ teaspoon Tabasco sauce
Salt and pepper to taste

Mix mustard and horseradish. Blend in vinegar until smooth. Add onions, Tabasco, salt, pepper and cream. Serve over boiled brisket or baked fish.

SOUR CREAM DRESSING

1 cup sour cream
1 teaspoon each of diced green peppers, minced parsley and minced onions
¾ cup catsup
1 tablespoon fresh horseradish
3 tablespoons olive oil
½ teaspoon paprika
1 tablespoon lemon juice

Season to taste with salt and red pepper. Mix well and use to cover shrimp, crab meat or oysters served in cocktail glass.

TONY'S HOLLANDAISE SAUCE

4 egg yolks
1 cup (2 sticks) butter or margarine
¼ teaspoon salt
Dash of red pepper
2 tablespoons lemon juice

Divide each stick of butter or margarine into 8 pieces. With a wooden spoon beat egg yolks in top of double boiler until smooth; blend in lemon juice. Place over simmering, not boiling, water.

Add butter or margarine, 1 piece at a time, stirring constantly until all the butter has been used and sauce has thickened. Season with salt and pepper and remove top of double boiler from water.

NOTE: Sauce can be made ahead of time and kept warm over simmering water. If sauce should separate, beat in a few drops of boiling water with a wooden spoon until sauce is smooth.

RAISIN SAUCE for BAKED HAM

1 cup brown sugar
1 or 2 tablespoons cornstarch
½ tablespoon salt
¼ teaspoon red pepper
1 tablespoon powdered mustard
Pinch of powdered mace, nutmeg and cinnamon
1 cup seedless raisins
½ cup white vinegar
3 cups water
½ teaspoon whole cloves

Mix dry ingredients, add raisins, vinegar and water. Cook to a syrup. Pour over sliced ham. Place in 300 degree oven for about 10 minutes and serve.

LAGNIAPPE

HOW TO COOK RICE

In a saucepan wash rice in cold water two or three times. Drain off, then add 1½ cups of water and ½ teaspoon of salt for each cup of rice. Cook over medium heat until water boils down to rice. Lower flame as low as possible, cover and let steam at least 15 minutes.

Another convenient way is to use a double boiler and let rice steam until cooked.

SALADS AND SALAD DRESSINGS

Two-piece Gift Box, containing large economy size **17 oz. Tony Chachere's Famous Creole Seasoning** and one sifter top box of **Instant Creole Gravy & Gumbo Mix. $6.50** per box, prepaid.

Three-piece Gift Box, containing **Tony Chachere's New Revised Cajun Country Cookbook, Creole Seasoning and Instant Creole Gravy & Gumbo Mix. $12.60** per box, prepaid.

Nine-piece Gift Box, containing **Tony Chachere's New Revised Cajun Country Cookbook, New Cajun Country MICRO-WAVE cookbook,** one 8 oz. sifter top box **Creole Seasoning,** one 10 oz. **Instant Creole Gravy & Gumbo Mix,** one 9 oz. **Creole Crab Boil,** one 10 oz. **Creole Seafood Sauce,** one 10 oz. **Creole Steak Sauce,** one 1¼ oz. bottle of **Creole Gumbo File** (Fee-lay), one 18 oz. bottle of **Creole Barbecue Sauce.** All in a ready-to-ship gift box. **$28.75** per box, prepaid.

OPELOUSAS FRENCH DRESSING

2 cups Wesson oil
1 cup olive oil
3 tablespoons Worcestershire sauce
1 tablespoon salt
2 tablespoons sugar
1 tablespoon salad mustard
6 cloves garlic, minced
½ cup minced scallions (tops and bottoms)
¼ cup minced parsley
½ teaspoon Tabasco sauce

Mix all ingredients and beat until emulsion results, or use blender.

CREOLE SALAD DRESSING

1 pint olive oil
4 ounces cider vinegar or wine vinegar
4 cloves garlic, mashed well
2 ounces water
1 teaspoon cornstarch
Tony's Creole Seasoning to taste

Dissolve cornstarch in vinegar, then add olive oil and garlic. Shake well until emulsified. Sprinkle lightly over lettuce or any salad you prefer. Season salad with Tony's Creole Seasoning to taste.

MAYONNAISE

1 teaspoon dry mustard
1 teaspoon salt
1 teaspoon sugar
Pinch red pepper
2 egg yolks
2 tablespoons lemon juice
2 cups salad oil or olive oil

Chill oil. Mix the dry ingredients into egg yolks and, when well mixed, add ½ teaspoon lemon juice. Add oil gradually, stir constantly. As mixture thickens, thin with lemon juice. Add oil and lemon juice, alternately until all is used, stirring or beating constantly. Oil added too rapidly will give dressing a curdled appearance. A smooth consistency may be restored by taking a yolk of another egg, adding curdled mixture to it slowly. (Makes about 2½ cups)

ROQUEFORT DRESSING

Mix 4 ounces of broken pieces of Roquefort cheese in ½ cup oil and 3 tablespoons of vinegar. Add sufficient amount of sour cream to make a thick dressing. Season to taste.

THE CAJUN WAY to ADD GARLIC to a SALAD

Use the nose of a French bread and rub with garlic vigorously all over. Cut in small squares and leave in the bottom of the bowl and toss salad.

MADGE'S SPINACH SALAD

1 small bunch fresh spinach (young, tender)
4 slices bacon
2 tablespoons tarragon vinegar
2 tablespoons white vinegar
Salt and pepper

Wash spinach leaves in cold water and dry. Place in mixing bowl. Fry bacon until crisp and crumble over spinach leaves. To bacon drippings, add vinegars and warm the mixture. When ready to serve, season spinach with salt and pepper to taste and pour above mixture over the leaves. Toss and serve. (Serves 4)

GREEN BEAN SALAD

2 large cans whole green beens
1 large onion, sliced
Several bits ham, bacon or smoked sausage
1 cup mayonnaise
2 hard-cooked eggs, chopped
1 heaping tablespoon horseradish (from the dairy case)
1 teaspoon Worcestershire
1 teaspoon chopped parsley
Tony's Creole Seasoning or salt and pepper
Juice of 1 lemon

Drain beans and add equal amount of water. In a heavy saucepan simmer beans with meat and onion for 1 hour or more. Blend mayonnaise with remaining ingredients and set aside at room temperature. When beans are ready to serve, drain and spoon mayonnaise mixture over vegetables. (Serves 8)

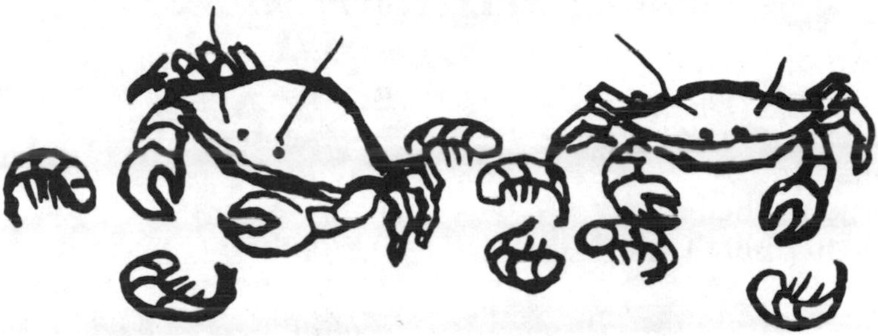

CRAB MEAT SALAD

1 pound white lump crab meat, fresh and ready to serve
1 head iceburg lettuce, broken in small chunks
8 ounces olive oil mayonnaise, freshly made
1 tablespoon capers, chopped fine
1 teaspoon lemon juice
Red pepper to taste
Parsley, chopped fine
Paprika

Place lump crab meat and small chunks of lettuce in a salad dish. Mix lemon juice, pepper and capers with mayonnaise and pour over crab meat and lettuce. Decorate with sprinklings of parsley and paprika. (Serves 6)

SHRIMP SALAD

1 pound boiled shrimp
2 sticks celery finely chopped
1 hard-boiled egg, finely chopped
1 sweet pickle, finely chopped
½ teaspoon capers, minced
2 tablespoons mayonnaise
Tony's Creole Seasoning to taste

Peel and devein shrimp and cut each one into 2 or 3 pieces. Add celery, egg, pickle, capers and mayonnaise. Mix thoroughly and add seasoning to taste. Serve on lettuce leaves or stuff into avocado or tomato halves. (Serves 4 to 6)

PARTY SHRIMP MOLD

1 envelope gelatin
¼ cup cold water
1 can tomato soup, undiluted
1 large package Philadelphia Cream Cheese
½ cup mayonnaise
½ cup whipped cream
½ cup chopped olives
1 tablespoon onion juice
1 tablespoon butter
Salt to taste
1 tablespoon Tabasco sauce
1 tablespoon Worcestershire sauce
1 cup chopped green peppers
½ cup chopped celery
1 pound boiled chopped shrimp

Heat the soup in double boiler, add cheese, onion juice and butter. While cheese is heating, mix gelatin and cold water. When cheese is heated and mixture is smooth, add gelatin mixture and cool. Then add shrimp, mayonnaise, whipped cream, olives and other ingredients. Pour into a wet mold or a mold greased with mayonnaise. Refrigerate for at least 2 hours. This may also be frozen.

TOMATO SHRIMP SALAD

4 large ripe tomatoes
1 pound boiled shrimp, diced
6 stuffed olives, chopped
2 tablespoons chopped onion
2 boiled eggs, chopped
1 cup olive oil mayonnaise, freshly made
Salt and pepper to taste
1 teaspoon lemon juice
2 tablespoons chopped celery

Hollow out tomatoes and fill with mixture of above ingredients. Serve on leaf of lettuce in salad dish. (Serves 4)

STUFFED AVOCADO SALAD

½ cup minced celery
1 cup crab meat
6 tablespoons salad dressing
3 avocados
Parsley for garnish

Mix crab meat, celery and salad dressing. Cut avocados in half and fill with mixture. Garnish with parsley and serve on lettuce leaf. (Serves 6)

TOMATO ASPIC

3 cups tomato juice
2 packages lemon gelatin
1 tablespoon plain gelatin
2 tablespoons Worcestershire sauce
4 tablespoons vinegar or lemon juice
Dash or two Tabasco
1 cup celery, chopped very fine
½ cup India relish
1 small bottle stuffed olives, sliced

Heat juice to boiling. Remove from heat, add lemon gelatin and plain gelatin, dissolve and let cool. Add Worcestershire, vinegar and Tabasco. When mixture begins to thicken add celery, olives and relish. Pour in mold and refrigerate until firm. (Serves 4)

CHERRY GELATIN SALAD

2 3-ounce packages gelatin desert (cherry)
1 Coke, 10-ounce size
1-No. 2 can crushed pineapple, drained
1 can black Bing cherries, pitted (drained)
8-ounce package cream cheese
1 cup nuts, chopped

Heat pineapple and cherry juice; add gelatin and dissolve. Add Coke, softened cream cheese, drained pineapple and cherries, and nuts. Mix well, pour in mold and chill in refrigerator until set. (Serves 8)

CHICKEN SALAD

1 large hen
1 stick celery, chopped fine
1 hard-boiled egg, chopped
4 hard-boiled egg whites, chopped
3 sour pickles, diced
Few capers, to taste, mashed
1 cup chicken broth
Mayonnaise

Boil hen until it begins to tender, add salt and pepper and a few cloves garlic (if desired). Remove chicken and debone. Cut breast into large pieces with scissors and put remaining parts through grinder. Add 1 cup chicken broth, then celery, egg, egg whites, pickles and capers. Let stand in refrigerator until chilled thoroughly. Add mayonnaise to taste. Serve on lettuce leaves. (Serves 8)

LIME GELATIN SALAD

½ 3-ounce size package lime gelatin
½ 3-ounce size package lemon gelatin
1 cup boiling water
½ No. 2 can crushed pineapple, drained
½ carton cottage cheese, (small size)
½ can condensed milk
½ cup finely chopped nuts
1 heaping tablespoon horseradish (from the dairy case)
1½ tablespoons lemon juice
Pinch of salt to taste
½ cup mayonnaise

Dissolve gelatin in hot water and let stand until cool. Add pineapple. Blend cheese with mayonnaise until smooth. Add gelatin mixture. Add all other ingredients and stir until mixture begins to congeal. Pour into individual molds and place in refrigerator overnight. (Serves 8)

HAROLD'S HAND SALAD

2 heads lettuce
4 tomatoes or 3 cups ripe cherry tomatoes
2 bunches parsley
2 bunches scallions (green onion tops)
2 cups small round radishes
10-ounce bottle pickled cauliflower
1 small jar stuffed olives with pimento
2 small jars hearts of artichokes
1 can ripe black olives
12 Italian pickled peppers
1 small bottle Italian salad dressing
1 small jar stuffed olives with almonds

Wash vegetables in cold water and drain. Break lettuce into bite size pieces. Chop parsley and cut scallions in 3-inch pieces. Dice tomatoes and cut radishes in half. Drain and discard juice of olives, artichokes, cauliflower and peppers. Put all ingredients in a large salad bowl. Season with salt and pepper to taste, add salad dressing (enough to barely coat) and toss with hands.

Set bowl in middle of table and let guests select favorite pieces with their fingers.

Keeps them happy before main meal is served.

GUMBOS AND SOUPS

LAGNAIPPE

How to Barbecue with Tony Chachere's

Creole Barbecue Sauce

How to Use The Sauce:

Add one stick of margarine or butter to each pint of barbecue sauce and heat in a saucepan until melted.

Tips for Real Creole Barbecuing:

First don't confuse charcoal broiling with barbecuing. Charcoal broiling is fast cooking on an open pit with heat and flame. Tony Chachere's barbecuing technique is to use a closed pit to regulate heat and create smoke for a slow smoking of the meat.

Secrets to Creole barbecuing: Proper seasoning, hickory chips, smoking and basting. (For tender spare ribs, beef or pork, boil in water 15 minutes before barbecuing.)

For The Best Flavor—

All types meat and poultry, use this recipe: Season meat the day before with Tony Chachere's Famous Creole Seasoning and put in refrigerator to marinate. Use hickory chips or sawdust soaked in water the day before—this prevents flaming and creates smoke. Light the charcoal. When coals become red, place chips on top of coals. Put seasoned meat on rack and close lid. There should be no flames, only smoke. Wait 10 minutes and check meat. If the meat is beginning to smoke, it should be reddish-brown and ready to turn. Repeat on other side. Use the oily top of barbecue sauce to baste. Repeat until meat is cooked to your taste. Serve the rest of the barbecue sauce over the meat or on the side.

The secret is the smoke and basting for the delicious flavor. Great for chicken, lamb, pork, and beef.

An All Purpose Sauce—

Delicious on hamburgers, hot dogs and steak sandwiches. (So good you'll hide it from the kids.)

GUMBO

Gumbo is a real Creole dish. It's served in a soup bowl with boiled **rice and garnished with file'(a must) sprinkled lightly on top.**

You can use any of the following to make a good gumbo: chicken, duck, goose, wild duck, quail, woodcock, dove, snipe or (best of all) guinea fowl, rabbit and squirrel. You can add sausage, tasso, andouille, smoked sausage and okra.

Seafood gumbos are made with shrimp, crabs, oysters and okra or either.

The basics are the same, except seafood takes about 30 minutes to cook, so add last.

FILE'

(Real Cajun Style)

File' (Fee-lay) — the finely-ground sassafras leaves which add such an exotic flavor to gumbo.

In the month of August, during the full moon, break branches (in fully- matured leaf) from sassafras tree. Hang branches to dry in shaded, ventilated place for about two weeks. Expose to bright sunlight 1 **to 1½ hours before finely-grinding in a mill. Store in amber jars** tightly sealed, in a cool place or in refrigerator for even longer-lasting quality.

If you're in a hurry, file' may also be found in a small jar at your grocer's or if you have the time, order my spiced Gumbo File' from the back of the book.

There is one thing about the Cajun — take away his roux, onions and bell pepper, his gumbo file' and he's lost.

CRAWFISH GUMBO

1 pound peeled crawfish tails
2 cups Basic Vegetable Mix (See page 5)
1 stick margarine
3 tablespoons flour
2 slices lemon
1 tablespoon Worcestershire sauce
1 quart water
1 bay leaf
¼ teaspoon thyme
¼ teaspoon basil

Use aluminum pot (do not use black iron pot). Melt margarine and make a brown roux with the flour, not too dark. Turn off burner and add Basic Vegetable Mix and saute until it stops sizzling. Add the water, return to burner, add Worcestershire sauce, lemon slices, and bay leaf, thyme and basil. Let come to a boil, simmer for at least 2 hours. Season with Tony's Creole Seasoning to taste. Add crawfish tails and fat, if you have some. Cook slowly for 40 to 50 minutes. (Serves 4)

TONY'S OYSTER CHOWDER

12-ounce jar fresh oysters
1 green bell pepper, chopped
1 large onion, chopped
1 stick celery, chopped
2 medium potatoes, diced
1 small bay leaf
¼ pound salt pork, diced
2½ cups milk
2 cups water
2 tablespoons flour
1 tablespoon chopped onion tops and parsley (for garnish)
Tony's Famous Creole Seasoning to taste

Cook green pepper in boiling water for 1 minute. Drain, rinse in cold water and drain again. In a large saucepan fry pork over gentle heat, stirring until brown. Add onions and celery and cook until golden brown; then add green pepper, potatoes, bay leaf and water and bring to a boil. Season and simmer 10 minutes or until potatoes are tender. Remove from heat.

Gradually add ½ cup milk to flour, stirring to form a smooth mixture. Blend into chowder. Return to heat and stir until boiling. Heat remaining milk and add to chowder along with the oysters and liquid. Simmer 5 minutes before serving. Sprinkle with onion tops and parsley. Serve in soup bowls with crackers. (Serves 4)

This is Cajun Country. No Yankees allowed. That includes Manhattan and New England.

SHRIMP and OKRA GUMBO

2 pounds fresh peeled shrimp
2 cups fresh diced okra
2 tablespoons oil
1 stick margarine
4 tablespoons flour
Tony's Creole Seasoning to taste
1 bell pepper
2 sticks celery
2 cloves garlic
1 tablespoon Worcestershire sauce
1 tablespoon chopped scallions
1 onion

Fry fresh okra in 2 tablespoons of oil for 10 minutes, stirring **constantly, so as not to burn. Use an aluminum Dutch oven, do not** use black iron pot. Remove okra and set aside. Add margarine and flour and make a roux in the same pot. Chop all vegetables, add them and the okra and cook for 5 minutes until wilted.

Add 3 quarts of water and Worcestershire sauce and cook 1 to 2 hours. Then add shrimp and cook 30 minutes or until tender, seasoning to taste with Tony's Creole Seasoning. Serve with boiled rice in a soup plate and garnish with onion tops and a sprinkling of filé.

SEAFOOD GUMBO

Make a roux with 1 cup flour and 1 cup oil. Set aside.

4 cleaned crabs and claws, cut in 4
2 pounds fresh peeled shrimp
½ pound fish fillets, cut in bite-size pieces
½ pint oysters
1 can whole tomatoes
1 stick margarine
½ cup chopped celery
Tony's Creole Seasoning to taste
½ cup chopped green bell peppers
4 cloves garlic, minced
3 quarts water
2 cups chopped okra (cooked)
1 tablespoon Worcestershire sauce
½ cup green onion tops and parsley, finely chopped
1 cup chopped onions

In a large aluminum Dutch oven or pot (not black iron pot) saute, in melted margarine, onions, celery, green bell pepper, garlic and okra for 10 minutes. Add to mixture roux, water and Worcestershire sauce and season to taste. Cook for 1 hour. Add all other ingredients, except onion tops and parsley, and cook for another hour.
Serve in soup plate with boiled rice, garnished with onion tops, parsley and dash of filé. (Serves 8)

GUINEA GUMBO

The guinea fowl is the No. 1 choice in Louisiana for flavor and taste.

3 pound guinea, dressed and drawn (save the liver, gizzard and heart)
1 stick margarine
4 tablespoons flour
½ cup cooking oil
1 onion, chopped
2 sticks chopped celery
1 green bell pepper, chopped
3 cloves garlic, chopped fine
1 tablespoon Worcestershire sauce
Tony's Creole Seasoning or salt and pepper
3 quarts cold water
Onion tops (scallions) and parsley, minced
File'

Cut up guinea hen in pieces and season with Tony's Creole Seasoning or salt and pepper. Fry in Dutch oven with cooking oil until slightly brown. Remove guinea.

Add margarine and flour to the Dutch oven, along with the drippings from the guinea, and make a brown roux. When the roux is completed, add onion (chopped), celery, bell pepper and garlic. **Stir well. Cut off fire, continue to stir until it stops sizzling. Then add the meat, Worcestershire sauce and 3 quarts of warm water. Let it come to a boil. Season to taste, and cook until meat is tender (2 to 3 hours). Skim off excess fat before serving.**

On each serving, sprinkle onion tops and parsley, plus dash of file'. Serve with boiled rice, French bread and a green salad. A good red wine is a must!

In place of guinea you may substitute chicken, duck, dove, squirrel, rabbit or what have you.

Some Cajuns like to add about ½ lb. diced, smoked pork sausage to gumbo.

I like to add a pint of fresh oysters, with the juice, about 10 minutes before serving.

CHICKEN and OKRA GUMBO

4 to 6 pound hen,
cut into pieces
4 tablespoons oil
1 stick margarine
4 tablespoons flour
2 cups chopped fresh okra
1 large onion, chopped
2 sticks celery, chopped
1 green bell pepper,
chopped
4 cloves garlic, minced
2 tablespoons chopped
green onions (scallions)
1 tablespoon
Worcestershire sauce
Tony's Creole Seasoning
or salt and pepper
3 quarts water
File'

Season chicken with Tony's Creole Seasoning or salt and pepper. In a large aluminum Dutch oven (do not use black iron pot) fry seasoned chicken in 2 tablespoons oil until brown. Remove and set aside. Add 2 more tablespoons oil and fry chopped okra for about 10 minutes, stirring constantly to keep from burning. Add a roux made with margarine and flour. Add chicken, Worcestershire sauce, chopped onion, celery, bell pepper, garlic and 3 quarts of warm water. Bring to a boil and simmer 2 or 3 hours or until meat is tender. Skim off excess fat and serve in soup bowls with rice. Garnish with chopped scallions and a sprinkling of file'. (Serves 10)

CREOLE BOUILLON (SOUP)

5 pounds of bouilli meat
(that's calf kidney, heart,
melt, sweetbreads and
brisket, cut in small
pieces)
4 onions, chopped
1 chopped green bell
pepper
4 sticks celery, chopped
4 pods garlic, minced
1 cup flour
2-No. 2 cans tomatoes
1 cup diced potatoes
1 can corn, whole kernel
1 can tomato paste
1 teaspoon sugar
4 quarts water
Tony's Creole Seasoning
or salt and pepper
1 cup salad oil

Make a roux with oil and flour. Add chopped vegetables and cook 5 minutes. Add meat, mix well and add all other ingredients. Add water and season to taste with Tony's Creole Seasoning or salt and pepper. Cook for 4 to 6 hours, adding more water if needed. If too thick omit roux or cut in half. (Serves 10)

CREOLE VEGETABLE SOUP

2 pounds heavy beef brisket or soup bone
1 large onion
Tony's Creole Seasoning or salt and pepper
2 ribs celery
1 large Irish potato
3 quarts water
1-No. 2 can tomatoes
1 cup chopped cabbage
3 carrots, chopped
2 sticks celery, chopped
½ onion, chopped
½ potato, chopped
2 sprigs parsley, minced
Small can of corn, whole kernel
2 tablespoons rice
Small amount broken spaghetti or macaroni
1 turnip, diced

In a 4-quart covered pot, boil meat in seasoned water with whole ribs of celery, whole onion and whole potato. Simmer for 3 hours or longer. Take soup meat from pot and remove meat from bone. Chop into bite-size pieces, discarding bone and fat.

Mash well-cooked vegetables through a strainer. Return these ingredients, with meat to the liquid. Add all other vegetables and rice; cook until vegetables are well done. Break small amount of spaghetti or macaroni into soup during last 20 minutes of cooking. (Serves 10)

DELICIOUS CORN SOUP

1 small brisket (about 1 pound)
½ cup chopped pickled pork (boiled to remove salt)
1 large onion, chopped
1 large can tomatoes
1 stick celery, chopped
6 or 8 ears fresh corn cut from cob

Put meat in Dutch oven, fill with water and let boil. Skim off foam, add tomatoes, onion and celery. Let simmer as you do for vegetable soup.

In a Dutch oven, smother cut corn in margarine until tender. After soup has simmered about 1 hour, and meat is tender, add corn and simmer another half-hour. (Serves 6)

CUCUMBER SOUP

6 tablespoons margarine
2 medium onions, chopped fine (or 1 cup)
2 large cucumbers, peeled and finely chopped (or 2 cups)
3 cups chicken stock, fresh or canned
2 tablespoons flour
2 egg yolks
½ cup heavy cream
1 medium-size cucumber, peeled and diced into ¼ inch pieces
Salt, white pepper
2 tablespoons minced parsley and green onion tops

In a heavy 2- or 3-quart saucepan melt 4 tablespoons margarine over moderate heat. When foam subsides, add onions and chopped cucumbers, stirring occasionally. Cook for about 5 minutes until onions are transparent, but not brown. Add chicken stock and bring to a boil. Lower heat and simmer, uncovered, for 20 to 30 minutes until vegetables are tender. Pour soup into a sieve set over a large bowl and force vegetables through with the back of a wooden spoon. Melt remaining 2 tablespoons margarine in a saucepan.

Remove pan from heat and stir in flour. Pour in soup puree, beating vigorously with a wire whisk. Return to moderate heat. Cook about 3 to 5 minutes, whisking constantly until soup has thickened slightly.

In a small bowl, combine egg yolks and cream. Beating constantly with a whisk, pour into it 1 cup of hot soup, 2 tablespoons at a time, then reverse the process. Slowly pour this mixture back into the remaining soup, still beating with the whisk. Simmer over very low heat 5 minutes, but do not let soup come to a boil.

Let soup cool to room temperature, then cover and refrigerate for at least 3 hours. Just before serving, add diced raw cucumber, seasoning, and sprinkle with parsley and green onion tops. Gently mix ingredients. (Serves 4)

NOTE: If preferred, you may serve the cold soup with a spoonful of slightly salted, stiffly whipped cream in each portion; or a spoonful of sour cream may be used.

TONY'S PINTO BEANS and SMOKED HAM HOCKS

1 2-lb. package pinto beans
4 smoked ham hocks
2 large onions, chopped
1 bell pepper, chopped
1 tablespoon Worcestershire sauce
6 cloves garlic, minced
Tony Chachere's Famous Creole Seasoning to taste (use half now and balance later to get right taste last)

Wash pinto beans in cold water. Use a 5 quart Dutch oven. Add all ingredients, except enough seasoning to taste. Fill pot with water. Bring to a boil and let boil slowly until meat falls from the bone and beans are tender. Bring seasoning up to taste and let boil until you have a fairly thick sauce. Ideal to pass around while cooking the main meal. (Makes about 20 small servings)

TONY'S LEEK SOUP

(Serve hot or cold)

6 leeks
1 tablespoon margarine
4 or 5 Irish potatoes, medium size
3 cups hot water
Salt to taste
1 cup light cream
1 cup hot milk
1 cup heavy cream
½ cup minced green onions (scallions)

Clean the white part of 6 leeks, cut them into enough small pieces (diced) to make 2 cups. Melt margarine in a heavy soup kettle; add leeks and cover the kettle. Cook leeks slowly, stirring occasionally, for a few minutes or until they are soft, but not brown. Peel and dice potatoes (enough to make 3 to 3½ cups). To the kettle, add potatoes, hot water and salt to taste. Cook the soup fully for 30 minutes or until the potatoes are very soft.

Strain the soup through a fine sieve or force it through a food mill. Return the strained puree to kettle and add light cream and hot milk. Bring soup to a boil, stirring occasionally to keep the puree from settling to the bottom and burning. Strain it again through a fine sieve. Cook soup, stirring occasionally, to keep smooth. Strain soup again; add heavy cream. Mix soup well, heat and serve, garnished with green onions; or mix the soup well and chill it thoroughly.

Garnish each serving with a sprinkling of green onions. Serve with toasted bread croutons. (Serves 6)

TONY'S CAS-CA-RA

3 pounds navy beans
1 pound boiled ham, diced
3 cups basic vegetable mix (see page 5)
1 stick margarine
Tony's Creole Seasoning

Boil navy beans in salted water until tender and strain through collander. Melt margarine and add vegetable mix. Saute for 10 minutes. Add diced ham and saute for another 10 minutes. Add strained navy beans and enough water to make a thick sauce. Season with Tony's Creole Seasoning to taste. Simmer for one hour. Add more water if needed. Serve in soup plates with crackers. (Serves 8)

BLACK BEAN SOUP

(Nassau)

2 cups black beans
2½ quarts cold water
2 sticks finely chopped celery
1½ large onions, minced
1 stick butter
2 bay leaves
1¼ tablespoons flour
¼ cup chopped parsley
1 ham hock and rind
1½ leeks, thinly sliced (or scallions)
Tony's Creole Seasoning to taste
½ cup Madeira wine or equal
1 hard-boiled egg, chopped

Wash beans, cover with cold water and soak overnight. Drain, add more water and cook over low heat for 1½ hours. In soup kettle, saute celery and onions in butter until tender. Blend in flour and parsley and cook 1 minute. Gradually stir in beans and liquid. Add ham hock, rind, leeks, bay leaves and Tony's Creole Seasoning to taste.

Simmer 4 hours over low heat. Remove ham hock, rind and bay leaves, and mash beans through sieve. Combine pureed beans and broth with Madeira wine; bring to boil. Remove from heat and add chopped eggs. Float a slice of lemon on each serving. (Serves 4 or 5)

TURTLE SOUP

140-year-old recipe

3 pounds turtle meat
4 quarts water
3 tablespoons flour
2 tablespoons shortening
2 medium onions, chopped
3 sticks celery, ground
6 pods garlic, ground
1 large green pepper, ground
Parsley
3 heaping tablespoons whole allspice (tied in thin cloth)
2 lemons sliced thin
4 tablespoons Worcestershire sauce
4 hard-cooked eggs
Tony's Creole Seasoning to taste
1 tablespoon sherry per serving

Boil turtle meat in water until tender. Remove scum which forms with spoon. Make roux using shortening and flour. Add ground celery, onions, garlic and bell pepper.

Remove turtle meat from stock, strain stock and add to roux. Bones may be removed from turtle meat. Add meat to stock along with lemons, Worcestershire sauce, and Tony's Creole Seasoning to taste.

Place bag of spices in soup and simmer for one hour. Add 1 tablespoon sherry per serving shortly before serving, if desired. Garnish with sliced hard-cooked eggs and parsley.

When in doubt season with Tony's Creole Seasoning and you'll never fail.

Whenever you make gumbo, soup or stew remember to skim off excess fat.

SEAFOOD

TONY'S CRAWFISH CASSEROLE

1 lb. peeled crawfish tails
2 cups cooked rice
3 slices bread (wet, wring, and tear apart)
1 can mushroom soup
1 cup chopped celery
⅓ cup chopped bell peppers
1½ cup chopped onions
3 cloves garlic, minced
½ cup onion tops, chopped
1 cup bread crumbs
1 stick oleo
1 teaspoon Tony Chachere's Famous Creole Seasoning

Season crawfish with Tony's Seasoning. Melt oleo in Dutch oven and saute crawfish for 5 minutes. Remove crawfish. Add all vegetables and saute for 10 minutes. Add all other ingredients, except bread crumbs. Place in casserole. Cover with bread crumbs and bake at 375 for 30 minutes.

TONY'S CRAB SOUP

1 lb. crab meat
1 large onion
2 cloves garlic
1 stick celery
1 teaspoon celery salt
1 teaspoon dry mustard
1 quart scalded milk
1 tablespoon cornstarch
2 tablespoons dry sherry
1 stick butter or oleo
¼ cup onion tops, chopped
1 cup croutons
Tony Chachere's Famous Creole Seasoning to taste

Melt butter in Dutch oven. Add all vegetables, finely chopped except onion tops. Saute for 5 minutes, add cornstarch and mustard and mix well. Add seasoned crab meat and cook for 3 minutes. Then slowly add hot milk and stir until mixture thickens. Simmer while stirring for 10 minutes. Add onion tops and serve in a soup bowl with croutons added. (Serves 4 to 6)

You can substitute chopped shrimp, lobster or crawfish.

TONY'S CRAWFISH COCKTAIL

1 pound peeled crawfish tails
1 cup Creole Seafood Cocktail Sauce (See page 14)
Tony's Creole Seasoning to taste

Season crawfish tails generously with Tony's Creole Seasoning. In a quart saucepan, place seasoned crawfish tails and two cups water, bring to a boil and boil slowly not more than 5 minutes. Drain and marinate in the Creole Seafood Sauce. Serve on lettuce leaves. (Makes 8 servings)

TONY'S CRAWFISH BOULETTES AND STUFFED SHELLS

1 pound peeled crawfish tails
1 onion, chopped
1 green bell pepper, chopped
2 sticks celery, chopped
2 cloves garlic, minced
1 tablespoon paprika
2 eggs
1 cup bread crumbs or corn bread
Tony's Famous Creole Seasoning or salt and pepper

Chop crawfish tails into 4 pieces. Finely chop vegetables (do not grind). Combine this mixture with raw eggs, paprika, bread crumbs or corn bread. Season with Tony's Famous Creole Seasoning or salt and pepper. If too dry, add water, if too soft, add bread crumbs. Stuff into cleaned crawfish shells, roll in flour and fry in 350-degree deep fat until they float.

If you can't get crawfish shells, make boulettes by forming into balls, 1½ to 2 inch size, roll in flour and fry the same way. Serve as hors d'oeuvres or use in bisque.

TONY'S CRAWFISH BISQUE

1 pound peeled crawfish tails
2 sticks margarine
4 level tablespoons flour
1 onion, chopped
1 stick celery, chopped
2 cloves garlic, minced
1/4 lemon, sliced
1/3 small can tomato paste
1 teaspoon sugar
1 tablespoon Worcestershire sauce
2 quarts warm water
1 tablespoon chopped green onion tops
1 tablespoon chopped parsley
Tony's Creole Seasoning or salt and pepper
24 fried stuffed crawfish shells or use boulettes (see page 41)

Make a roux with flour and margarine in aluminum Dutch oven (do not use black iron pot - will cause crawfish to darken.) Cut off fire and add all chopped vegetables, except green onion tops. Stir until it stops sizzling. Add tomato paste, Worcestershire sauce, sugar and crawfish tails. Saute for 5 minutes. Add 2 quarts warm water, bring to a boil. Cut fire and simmer for 2 hours. Add stuffed crawfish shells if available or crawfish "boulettes" and cook another hour. Season with Tony's Famous Creole Seasoning to taste, or salt and pepper.

Serve in soup bowls over boiled rice and place 6 stuffed shells or 6 boulettes in each bowl. Garnish with onion tops and parsley. (Serves 4)

TONY'S FRIED CRAWFISH TAILS

1 pound peeled crawfish tails
1 small can Carnation milk
1 tablespoon Calumet baking powder
2 tablespoons vinegar
1 cup flour
Tony's Creole Seasoning
Oil for frying
2 eggs

Mix eggs, milk, baking powder and vinegar. Season crawfish tails and marinate in mixture at least 1 hour. Remove, dip each crawfish tail in flour and fry in 380-degree fat until brown. (Makes 4 servings)

TONY'S CRAWFISH ETOUFFEE

(pronounced A-too-fay)

1 pound peeled crawfish tails
1 stick margarine
1 medium onion, chopped
½ green bell pepper, chopped
1 tablespoon Worcestershire sauce
2 cloves garlic
2 tablespoons cornstarch
1 tablespoon paprika
1 tablespoon chopped onion tops
2 cups water
Tony's Famous Creole Seasoning or salt and pepper to taste

Use shrimp if you can't get crawfish.

Melt margarine in aluminum Dutch oven (don't use iron pot as black iron pot will cause crawfish to darken.) Season crawfish tails generously with Tony's Creole Seasoning or salt and pepper. Add paprika to margarine. Saute crawfish tails about 5 minutes. Remove crawfish and set aside.

To pot add onions, bell pepper and garlic. Saute well at least 10 minutes. Return crawfish tails to pot and add 2 cups water and Worcestershire sauce. Stir and simmer slowly about 40 minutes. Check for taste, add more seasoning if necessary. Add mixture of cornstarch and water slowly until slightly thickened.

Serve with rice and garnish with onion tops and parsley. (Serves 4)

TONY'S CRAWFISH STEW EMILE

1 pound peeled crawfish tails
1 stick margarine
3 tablespoons all-purpose flour
1 medium onion
1 medium bell pepper
2 sticks celery
1 clove garlic
1 tablespoon Worcestershire sauce
1 tablespoon chopped onion tops
Tony's Creole Seasoning or salt and pepper

Make a roux with margarine and flour in an aluminum Dutch oven (do not use black iron pot). When chocolatey, not brown, cut off fire and add all vegetables, chopped, and Worcestershire sauce. Stir mixture until it stops sizzling, add seasoned crawfish and enough water to cover all ingredients. Let simmer 30 minutes to 1½ hours (Use judgment). Serve with boiled rice, garnished with onion tops. (Makes 4 generous servings)

NOTE: More crawfish can be added without altering ingredients. You can also substitute shrimp, crab meat, oysters, clams or even fish fillets and get excellent results.

CRAWFISH CREPES

This is an original recipe as prepared by Executive Chef Hans John of the Shamrock Hilton, Houston, Texas. We pass it on to you with his blessing.

FILLING

1 cup cooked cleaned crawfish
1/4 cup chopped onion
1/2 cup sliced fresh or canned mushrooms
1 - 2 cups cream sauce

SEASONING

Salt, pepper, Tabasco, L & P sauce
1 - 2 tablespoons white wine

Saute onion, mushroom in small amount of butter or oleo. Add crawfish and wine. Simmer until liquid is reduced to half. Add cream sauce and seasoning.

CREPE

1 cup flour
2 whole eggs
Pinch salt
1 cup water
1 cup milk
2 tablespoons melted butter or salad oil

Mix all dry ingredients together. Add eggs and melted butter. Mix milk and water and stir in flour until smooth. Fill crepes and top with hollandaise and glaze.

TONY'S CRAWFISH PIE

1 unbaked pie shell and top
1 pound crawfish tails, peeled
1 can cream of mushroom soup
2 cups Basic Vegetable Mix (See page 5)
Tony's Creole Seasoning to taste
1/2 stick margarine

Saute crawfish tails in margarine about 5 minutes. Remove crawfish tails, add Basic Vegetable Mix to margarine and saute for 10 minutes. Season crawfish and add to mixture, along with the soup. Cook at least 20 minutes. If too thick, add a little Sauterne wine or water. Place in pie shell and cover with top. Bake in 300-degree oven until brown. (Serves 4)

TONY'S CRAWFISH EGG ROLLS

FILLING

½ cup finely chopped celery
¾ cup shredded cabbage
3 tablespoons oil
1 cup diced, cleaned crawfish tails
4 scallions (green onion tops), finely chopped
1 clove minced garlic
¼ cup soy sauce
½ cup water chestnuts, drained and finely chopped

Boil celery and cabbage in ½ cup of water. Drain. Heat oil in skillet, add crawfish and fry for 3 minutes, stirring constantly. Add remaining ingredients and fry for 5 minutes, stirring all the while. (Ham, beef, veal, chicken, shrimp, etc., may be substituted for crawfish.)

SKINS

¾ cup sifted flour
1 tablespoon cornstarch
2 eggs, beaten
Sugar (pinch)
¼ cup oil
1 teaspoon salt

Sift flour, cornstarch and salt in a bowl. Beat eggs and sugar and add 1½ cups water slowly. Beat constantly until batter is smooth. To make egg roll skins grease a hot 8 inch skillet with 1 teaspoon oil. Pour about 3 tablespoons batter into skillet, tipping skillet to spread batter over bottom. Fry over medium heat until batter shrinks from sides of skillet. Turn skin and fry for 1 minute on the other side. Remove and cool. (Makes 12 skins)

COOKING THE CRAWFISH EGG ROLLS

12 Crawfish Egg Roll Skins
1 recipe of crawfish egg roll filling
1 tablespoon flour
½ cup oil

Place 4 tablespoons filling in center of each skin. Fold two sides over edges of filling and roll up the skin. Seal with paste made from flour and 2 tablespoons water. Fry in oil until golden brown. Serve with Chinese Mustard Sauce, Page 15, and Chinese Brown Sauce, Page 14. (Serves 6)

HEAVENLY EGGS CRAWFISH

3 tablespoons butter or margarine
¼ cup milk or pure cream
¼ bell pepper, chopped fine
Salt and black pepper
8 eggs
1 small onion, chopped
3 scallions, chopped (green onion tops)
½ pound peeled crawfish tails

Saute crawfish, onions, bell pepper in butter until soft. Add beaten eggs and milk. Pour over mixture and cook until moisture has nearly evaporated and eggs are soft. Season with salt, black pepper and serve. (Serves 4)

NOTE: Shrimp, crab meat or lobster can be used in place of crawfish.

GUIDRY'S FRIED STUFFED HARD SHELL CRABS

1 dozen crabs, cleaned with claws removed
1 cup crab meat
1 stick margarine
2 onions, chopped
1 chopped bell pepper
2 sticks celery, chopped
2 pods garlic, chopped
2 eggs
1 cup milk
1 cup bread crumbs
1 cup corn meal
Tony's Creole Seasoning or salt and pepper

Season crabs with Tony's Creole Seasoning or salt and pepper and set aside. Melt margarine and saute crab meat, onions, celery, bell pepper and garlic until brown. Add one raw egg, mixed with bread crumbs. Mix well and season to taste. Stuff body cavities of crabs with the mixture. Dip crabs in egg and milk mixture, roll in corn meal and fry in deep fat (375 degrees) until brown. (Serves 4)

TONY'S SECRET TO COOKING LIVE CRAWFISH, SHRIMP AND CRAB

I perfer to steam my seafood because it uses less seasoning and takes less time, besides it tastes much better. To steam seafood, add three inches of water, regardless of size of pot. USE NO SEASONING. Cover pot tightly, and when steam comes out of the top add a basket full of seafood (regardless of weight). Replace top tightly so that steam will bubble over seafood. When steam comes out of top again start timing, 5 minutes for crawfish, 4 minutes for shrimp and 10 minutes for crabs. Have a styrofoam chest ready to add a layer of seafood then a layer of Tony Chachere's Famous Creole Seasoning or Crab Boil. Layer by layer. Cover chest tightly and let stand 10 minutes. Seafood will stay hot up to five hours. Add a little oil or oleo to seafood when boiling or steaming. They'll peel lots easier.

CAUTION: Use only only styrofoam chest. Plastic or other chest will warp if used.

If you have a problem use our Toll Free Number, **1-800-551-9066.**

FRIED SOFT SHELL CRABS

6 soft shell crabs
1 egg
1 cup milk
1 cup flour
Salt and pepper to taste
Lemon slices and chopped parsley

Remove the soft feelers or "dead man" under each side of the shell. Remove eyes, mouth and sandbag under mouth. Wash crabs well in cold water and dry on paper towel.

Mix milk and egg and season with salt and pepper. Soak crabs in this mixture for one hour. Roll in flour and fry in deep fat fryer for 20 minutes or until reddish brown. Garnish with lemon slices and chopped parsley and serve with Tartar sauce. (Serves 6)

BOILED CRABS in a CHEST

Tony's Creole Seasoning or 1 box salt mixed with 4-ounce bottle red pepper
4 dozen live crabs
1 ice chest big enough to hold 4 dozen crabs

Plunge crabs in boiling water, boil for 11 minutes. Remove and immediately place (while hot) 1 layer crabs in bottom of ice chest. Sprinkle generously with seasoning, then place another layer of crabs. Season and repeat process until all crabs are placed and covered with seasoning. Cover with newspaper and close top securely. Heat will steam crabs and melt seasoning for flavor. After 1 hour, take out and eat. Crabs will keep hot for 5 or 6 hours. (Serves 8)

NOTE: You can do this with crawfish or shrimp the same way. Use a styrofoam chest; it will not warp.

BROILED SOFT SHELL CRABS

8 soft shell crabs
8 slices toast
½ cup butter
1 teaspoon parsley
1½ tablespoons oil
¼ teaspoon cayenne
2 lemons, thinly sliced
½ teaspoon salt

Clean crabs, drop them in oil, salt and pepper. Have broiler hot — 500 degrees; cook 10 minutes. Serve on toast with melted butter, parsley and sliced onions.

STUFFED CRAB SHELLS

2 cups crab meat
2 tablespoons onions, minced
1 cup bread crumbs
¼ pound butter
¼ cup water
Juice of ½ lemon
1 tablespoon parsley, chopped
2 hard-boiled eggs, minced

Brown onions in butter. Add crab meat, ½ cup bread crumbs, water and lemon juice. Cook for 15 to 20 minutes. Add parsley, minced eggs and fill the shells. Sprinkle with bread crumbs, place in baking dish and put in brisk oven for a few minutes. (Makes about 8 servings)

OPELOUSAS BARBECUED CRABS

1 dozen fresh cleaned crabs
1 cup chili powder
1 cup black pepper
1/3 cup salt
1 stick margarine
14-ounce bottle catsup
Juice of 1 lemon
1 teaspoon Tabasco
A few drops of liquid smoke

Roll cleaned crabs in mixture of equal parts, by weight, salt, black pepper and fresh chili powder. Fry in deep fat, 375 degrees, until they float, about seven minutes.

Make a sauce with melted margarine or butter, catsup, lemon juice, Tabasco and a few drops of liquid smoke. Pour this sauce over the crabs and serve hot. (Serves 2)

CRAB MEAT and GREEN PEPPERS

2 cups cooked crab meat
6 green peppers
1 cup light cream
4 tablespoons butter
1/4 teaspoon ground nutmeg
2 tablespoons cornstarch
1 teaspoon lemon juice
1/4 cup dry white wine
1 cup cooked rice
Paprika
1 teaspoon salt

Cut tops off peppers and remove seeds. Parboil peppers 5 minutes, drain. Scald cream, add butter and nutmeg. Mix cornstarch, wine, lemon juice and salt. Add to cream. Cook until thickened, stirring constantly. Combine with crab meat and rice, and spoon into peppers. Sprinkle with paprika. Bake in greased baking dish in a moderate oven, 350 degrees, for 20 minutes. (Serves 6)

OPELOUSAS OYSTER LOAF

1 loaf French bread, unsliced
1 dozen select oysters, large
1 cup bread crumbs
Salt and pepper
1 egg
½ cup cream
1 cup cooking oil
Dill pickles
Lemon
Catsup
Butter

Cut off top of the French bread and reserve. Scoop out insides and toast the loaf. Butter inside generously and keep warm. Dry oysters in paper toweling.

Beat egg with salt and pepper, slowly adding cream. Place oysters in egg mixture, then in bread crumbs, thoroughly covering all sides. Fry in shallow oil until brown and drain on absorbent paper.

Fill the hollow of French loaf with the fried oysters. Garnish with sliced dill pickles, lemon wedges and dabs of catsup. Replace top, heat in oven, and serve. (Serves 4)

OYSTERS POULETTE

3 dozen fresh oysters
2 tablespoons margarine
2 tablespoons flour
2 shallots (green onions or scallions), chopped
1 cup oyster liquid or bouillon
4 egg yolks
1 cup cream
2 tablespoons lemon juice
1 tablespoon minced parsley
Tony's Creole Seasoning or salt and pepper
Bread crumbs, buttered

In a saucepan heat oysters to draw out juice. Remove oysters, skim juice and reserve. Melt margarine and add flour, stirring until smooth. Add shallots and cook until wilted. Add oyster liquid or bouillon and blend well. Add seasoning, egg yolks beaten with cream, oysters, parsley and cook 2 minutes. Remove from fire, add lemon juice. Place in a casserole or individual shells and sprinkle with bread crumbs. Heat in oven just before serving. (Serves 3 to 6)

OYSTERS ROCKEFELLER

6 dozen oysters
3 dozen oyster half-shells
Juice of 1 lemon
½ teaspoon anise seed
1 tablespoon anisette or Herbsaint
½ cup minced parsley
2 cloves garlic, chopped
2 12-ounce boxes frozen chopped spinach
1 teaspoon Dijon Creole mustard
1½ sticks margarine
1 teaspoon Tabasco sauce
Salt and black pepper to taste
2 anchovies
Bread crumbs, enough to thicken
½ cup grated Parmesan cheese
6 pie pans half-filled with rock salt

Place oysters in a collander, drain juice into a pot and add equal amount of water to oyster juice. Cook juice until back to original amount. Blend vegetables, anchovies, anise seed and oyster liquid in a blender until smooth. Combine all ingredients, except oysters, in a saucepan and cook 40 minutes over medium heat; thicken with bread crumbs as needed. After cooking is complete, turn off fire and add anisette or Herbsaint.

In 500-degree oven, heat shells on rock salt, 6 shells to each pie pan. When hot, remove from oven and place 2 oysters on each shell, cover with sauce and sprinkle with mixture of equal parts Parmesan cheese and bread crumbs. Return to oven and bake 15 minutes. Serve hot. (Serves 6)

NOTE: You can substitute cherry stone clams for oysters.

OYSTERS en BROCHETTE

3 dozen select oysters
1 stick margarine
6 slices bacon
1 cup bread crumbs
Tony's Creole Seasoning or salt and pepper
6 skewers, 6 inches long

Cut bacon in pieces same length as oysters; alternate pieces of bacon and oyster on skewer, 6 on each. Season to taste. Dip filled skewer in bread crumbs, then in melted margarine. Broil for 5 or 10 minutes until bacon is crisp or cook over hot coals. Serve with toast and Tartar sauce. (Serves 3)

NOTE: Scallops and clams can be used instead of oysters.

OYSTERS BIENVILLE

6 pastry shells (size to hold 6 oysters)
36 small fresh oysters
1 stick margarine
4 tablespoons flour
1 pint Half and Half coffee cream
4-ounce can mushrooms
½ cup chopped, boiled shrimp
¼ cup chopped parsley
¼ cup medium chopped onions
¼ cup dry white wine
6 egg yolks
½ teaspoon thyme
¼ cup grated Parmesan cheese
Tony's Creole Seasoning to taste

Melt margarine in Dutch oven. Add flour, stir for 2 minutes; add preheated cream, stirring until thickened. Then add all ingredients except egg yolks and oysters. Stir well until cheese is melted. Do not overheat. Remove from fire and slowly add beaten egg yolks, stirring constantly.

Heat oysters in a separate saucepan until slightly shriveled. Pour off juice and reserve. Stir oysters into mixture and cook 5 minutes, adding oyster juice if too thick, season to taste.

Place 6 oysters in each pastry shell. Put shells in a shallow baking pan and fill with sauce. Place in 400-degree oven until hot. Serve immediately. (Serves 6)

OYSTER STEW

2 or 3 dozen small oysters with liquid
6 green onions, (scallions) chopped fine
1 rib of celery, chopped fine
2 sprigs parsley, minced
1 quart milk
1 stick butter or margarine
2 tablespoons flour
Salt and pepper
Worcestershire sauce
Slices of toast bread cut into croutons

Saute chopped vegetables in margarine and flour. Drain oysters and add liquid to vegetables. Add pre-heated milk, then oysters and simmer until oysters are plump and edges begin to turn. Add salt, pepper. Worcestershire sauce to taste. Serve with croutons. Sprinkle with parsley. (Serves 4)

HUITRES au DIABLE

(Deviled Oysters)

3 dozen oysters
1 tablespoon margarine
2 tablespoons flour, finely creamed
1 cup cream
2 egg yolks, well beaten
1 tablespoon minced parsley
1 bay leaf, crushed
1 sprig thyme, crushed
Salt and cayenne to taste
Bread crumbs
Sprigs of parsley, sliced lemons and olives to garnish

Take 3 dozen fine large oysters, drain and chop them into middling fine pieces. Rub together 1 tablespoon of margarine and 2 tablespoons of flour until smooth. Place cream in a saucepan and when it starts to boil stir in the margarine and flour. Have ready the yolks of eggs and as soon as the cream boils, take it from the fire; let it cool a little and add the eggs, parsley, bay leaf and thyme. Add salt and cayenne to taste and add the oysters.

Take the washed deep shells of the oysters, and fill with this mixture. Sprinkle lightly with bread crumbs and top with a pinch of margarine. Set in a baking pan and brown for 5 minutes in a very hot oven—500 degrees. Serve the baked oysters, in their shells and garnish the dish with sprigs of parsley, olives and sliced lemon. (Serves 6)

FROG MAN

George B. Marks, of Opelousas, is an expert frog hunter. He once caught 76 frogs in one hour. They weighed over 100 pounds. Friends call him the "Human Salamander". He crawls on lilies, catches them with his bare hands. Has a sack on his back, headlight on his head and uses two poles 6 feet long to crawl with.

FRIED FROGS

12 frog legs
½ cup lemon juice
1 teaspoon salt
2 eggs
1 cup sifted bread crumbs
1 cup chopped parsley
Oil for frying
Salt and pepper
Sliced lemons and parsley to garnish

Scald frog legs about 3 minutes in boiling water, containing ½ cup lemon juice and salt. Remove, dry with clean towel and season with Tony's Creole Seasoning or salt and pepper. Dip in a batter made of 2 well beaten eggs, then roll in bread crumbs. Cover frogs well and drop in oil heated to boiling point. Fry to a golden brown. Remove from oil and drain well on absorbent paper.

Fry parsley for 1 minute. Place a folded white napkin in a dish, lay frog legs upon it and garnish with fried parsley and sliced lemon; or place frog legs in a bed of fried parsley and garnish with parsley and slices of lemon. (Serves 6)

FROG LEGS with TARTAR SAUCE

24 pairs of frog legs (use small frog legs) (Japanese)
½ teaspoon salt
4 tablespoons paprika
1½ cups flour
Vegetable oil or shortening for deep frying
2 cups milk

Gently split frog legs apart and wash under cold running water. Blot thoroughly dry with a paper towel. In a small bowl mix together milk, salt and 2 tablespoons of paprika. Soak frog legs in mixture for about 5 minutes. Combine flour and remaining paprika and place it on a sheet of waxed paper.

In a heavy 12-inch skillet heat the oil, about 2 inches deep, over high heat until a light haze forms. Dip frog legs in the seasoned flour. Shake loose excess flour and fry legs in hot oil for about 5 minutes, turning them frequently with tongs. Regulate heat so that legs brown quickly without burning. Remove when golden brown and drain on paper towels. Serve hot with Tartar Sauce. (Serves 8)

FROG LEGS a la SAUCE PIQUANTE

8 frog legs
8 tablespoons flour
¾ cup shortening
1 medium sized onion, sliced thin
2 cloves garlic, minced fine
1 large can tomatoes
Water
Tony's Creole Seasoning or salt and pepper
Parsley and green onion tops (scallions), cut fine

Heat shortening and fry the frog legs after rolling them in flour. When well done, remove legs and add balance of flour to shortening and stir until golden brown. Add garlic, onions and stir until both are wilted. Add tomatoes and stir until oil floats on top. Add water to desired consistency and season highly. Place frog legs in this mixture and cook for 10 more minutes. Add parsley and onion tops just before serving. (Serves 4)

TONY'S BROILED LOUISIANA FROGS

12 whole frogs, cleaned and dressed
1 cup milk
2 sticks butter or margarine
¼ cup lemon juice
1 quart water
2 tablespoons chopped parsley
Tony's Creole Seasoning to taste

Scald frogs in the lemon juice and boiling water. Remove, dry and dip in milk. Season with Tony's Creole Seasoning and place in baking dish.

Cover frogs with cut up chips of butter and place in 400-degree broiler. Turn over when brown, baste and cook 10 to 20 minutes until brown.

Garnish with chopped parsley and serve with Tartar Sauce and toast. (Serves 6)

FROG LEGS PROVENCAL

- 3 pounds frog legs
- 1 cup butter
- 1 can tomato sauce
- 1 cup sliced mushrooms
- ¼ cup chopped parsley
- 2 cloves garlic, minced
- 1 cup heavy cream
- 1 cup flour
- 1 cup olive oil

Melt butter in a skillet and add tomato sauce, mushrooms, parsley, garlic and simmer for 10 minutes.

Dip frog legs in cream, then in flour. In other skillet saute legs in oil for 10 minutes or until brown. Serve with sauce. (Serve 6)

TURTLE STEW

(120-year-old recipe)

- 3 pounds turtle meat
- 3 tablespoons cooking oil or margarine
- 3 tablespoons flour
- 3 medium onions, chopped
- 2 cloves garlic, minced
- 2-No. 2 cans tomatoes
- 1 can tomato paste
- Boiling water
- 1 stick celery, chopped fine
- 1 bunch green onions, chopped fine
- 2 green bell peppers chopped fine
- 1 cup sherry wine
- ½ dozen hard-boiled eggs
- Tony's Creole Seasoning or salt and pepper
- 4 bay leaves
- 8 whole cloves
- ½ teaspoon allspice, powdered
- 1 tablespoon sugar
- ¼ lb. butter
- 1 lemon, sliced

Parboil the turtle meat. Make a brown roux of oil and flour. Add onions, garlic, bell pepper, tomato paste and tomatoes. Cook slowly 20 to 30 minutes. Add mixture to turtle meat, along with enough boiling water to cover meat. Boil down. Add celery, green onions, Tony's Creole Seasoning, wine, bay leaves, cloves, allspice and sugar.

Cook, covered, over high heat for 30 minutes. Mash egg yolks, chop the whites. Add to stew. If stew gets too thick, add a little water. Cook slowly for about 3 hours. One-half hour before serving, add sliced lemon and butter. (Serves 6)

NOTE: To increase amount, add ½ pound of turtle meat per person.

McJUNKINS TURTLE SAUCE PIQUANTE

George McJunkins is a redneck from Arkansas who migrated to Louisiana about 40 years ago. He rode into Port Barre, Louisiana on a borrowed mule and married a Cajun girl. Now he's considered a full fledged Cajun. Once they drink bayou water, they never leave.

3 pounds turtle meat, cut up
2 cups Basic Vegetable Mix (see page 5)
1 small can mushroom buttons
1 small can mushroom steak sauce
1 can Rotel tomatoes
2 teaspoons Worcestershire sauce
Tony's Creole Seasoning to taste
1 long green hot pepper, chopped
½ cup onion tops, chopped
¼ cup parsley, chopped

Boil meat for a few minutes. Drain and season with Tony's Creole Seasoning. Melt margarine in Dutch oven and brown meat until bottom starts to stick. Add chopped vegetable mix and cook for 10 minutes. Add mushrooms, steak sauce, Rotel and green hot peppers and about a pint of water. Bring to a boil; lower fire, cover pot and simmer for 3 to 4 hours until meat is tender.

If gravy is too thin make a mixture of a tablespoon of flour and cup of water. Cook until it thickens then add onion tops and parsley and serve. (Makes 6 servings)

CLAUDE'S TURTLE on the BAYOU

4 pounds turtle meat, cleaned and cut in small pieces
6 cloves of garlic, chopped fine
Tony's Creole Seasoning or salt and pepper
1 large onion, chopped fine

Add a small amount of cooking oil in a Dutch oven. Fry meat well and dredge with a little flour. Add onions, garlic and small amounts of cold water as needed. Watch the pot closely and keep stirring with just enough heat to simmer. Cook about 2 hours until the meat is tender. Serve with rice.

You get only a small amount of gravy here, but the meat and gravy on rice is out of this world. Claude likes yellow-bellied turtle for this. A good eater can hurt himself on this dish. (Serves 8)

BLACK PEPPER SHRIMP

2 pounds headless fresh shrimp unpeeled
2 sticks margarine
2-ounce can ground black pepper

Place shrimp in a baking pan and completely cover with the black pepper, then with sliced margarine. Cover and bake in 400-degree oven until shrimp turn red. Turn over once and cook the other side. When done, mix in juices and serve hot.

When peeled, they get the flavor of black pepper but not the hot taste.

Try this on your friends, you won't be disappointed. (Serves 4)

BROILED SHRIMP a la TONY

12 large unshelled shrimp
1 clove garlic, cut fine
1 teaspoon salt
½ teaspoon black pepper
1 cup olive oil
2 tablespoons lemon juice

Slit unshelled shrimp down back, cutting ¾ way through to remove sand veins. Marinate shrimp for 2 hours in mixture of remaining ingredients. Place shrimp in a broiling pan and pour marinade over shrimp. Broil 7 or 8 minutes, turning once. Use as appetizer. (Serves 4)

SHRIMP and EGGPLANT JAMBALAYA

1 medium eggplant
1 cup rice
1 can whole tomatoes
1 pound shrimp, cleaned
½ cup chopped onions
½ cup chopped celery
½ cup chopped green bell pepper
1 large spoon cooking oil
Salt and pepper
1 clove garlic, chopped

Peel and dice eggplant and fry in oil. When tender add onions, celery, bell pepper, garlic and cook a few minutes. Add tomatoes, and well-washed rice. Season to taste and let it all cook slowly for about 1 hour, adding water if needed. About 20 minutes before serving add the shrimp and cook until done. (Serves 6)

SHRIMP CHINESE STYLE

2 cups peeled shrimp
2 green bell peppers, sliced
1 teaspoon onion juice
4 tablespoons butter
4 tablespoons flour
1 teaspoon salt
1/8 teaspoon black pepper
2 cups milk
1 teaspoon soy sauce
4 tomatoes, quartered
Paprika

Saute peppers with onion juice in butter until soft, but not brown. Remove peppers from fat. Stir flour into butter, with salt and pepper, until well blended. Add milk slowly and cook, stirring constantly, until thickened. Add soy sauce, quartered tomatoes, peppers and shrimp. Cook over very low heat, stirring occasionally, for 10 minutes. Pour into serving dish, sprinkle with paprika and serve hot with hot steamed rice. (Serves 6)

CHINESE SKILLET SHRIMP

1 can pineapple chunks (1 1/4 pounds)
2 tablespoons peanut oil or equal
1 cup chopped celery
1 medium-size green bell pepper, cut in chunks
1/2 cup chopped green onions (scallions)
1 pound cooked shrimp
2 tablespoons soy sauce
2 tablespoons cornstarch
1/8 teaspoon powdered ginger
1/2 teaspoon garlic salt
1 cup chopped tomatoes or small tomatoes halved

Drain pineapple, reserving all syrup. Heat oil in a heavy skillet and saute celery and green pepper chunks until they turn bright green. Add shrimp, tossing with greens until heated through. Add pineapple chunks and green onions. Combine reserved pineapple syrup, soy sauce, cornstarch, ginger and garlic salt. Stir into shrimp mixture until thickened and bubbly. Add tomatoes and serve at once. (Serves 4)

SHRIMP FRIED RICE

2 cups chopped cooked shrimp
2 tablespoons soy sauce
4 cups boiled rice
¼ cup oil
2 eggs, lightly beaten
4-ounce can mushrooms
1 teaspoon salt
Freshly ground black pepper
½ cup scallions, chopped

Fry shrimp in oil in deep frying pan for 1 minute, stirring constantly. Add eggs, mushrooms, salt and pepper, and fry over medium heat for 5 minutes, stirring constantly. Add rice and soy sauce and fry for 5 minutes, stirring frequently. Mix with chopped scallions. (Serves 6)

Diced cooked chicken, pork or ham may be used instead of shrimp (or all of these for a fantastic taste sensation).

SHRIMP KEE KEE

1 cup cooked, shelled shrimp
2 tablespoons butter
Salt and pepper
Pinch of oregano
⅓ cup dry white vermouth
1¼ to 1½ cups milk
½ teaspoon salt
Pinch each of pepper and nutmeg
1 tablespoon tomato paste
¼ cup grated Swiss cheese
8 patty shells
3 eggs

Toss shrimp in melted butter over moderately high heat. Season lightly with salt, pepper and oregano. Add vermouth and boil rapidly until liquid has almost evaporated. Spread shrimp equally in bottom of patty shells. Beat together milk, eggs and seasoning. Add tomato paste and pour over shrimp, filling shell to ⅛ inch from top. Spread grated cheese on top and dot with butter. Bake 25 to 30 minutes at 375 degrees. (Serves 4)

PAT HUVAL'S (HENDERSON, LA) FRIED SHRIMP

So tender they melt in your mouth!

1 pound fresh shrimp (26 to 30 to a pound)
1 small can Carnation milk
2 eggs
1 tablespoon Calumet baking powder
2 tablespoons vinegar
1 cup flour
Tony's Creole Seasoning to taste

Remove head and shell from shrimp but leave fantail. Split shrimp down back and remove vein.

Make a mixture of eggs, Carnation milk, baking powder and vinegar. Marinate shrimp for at least 1 hour in this mixture. Remove, season lightly with Tony's Creole Seasoning. Dip in flour and fry in 380-degree fat, not over 10 minutes. (3 to 4 servings)

SMOKED FISH

8 bass fillets (or other)
½ cup lemon juice
1 cup olive oil
1 tablespoon Worcestershire
Tony's Creole Seasoning to taste
1 stick butter
2 tablespoons dry mustard
Basil leaves, bay leaves and thyme

Marinate fillets in mixture of lemon juice, Worcestershire sauce, Tony's Creole Seasoning to taste, and olive oil for 1 hour. Place fillets on wire rack in barbecue pit over low coals and hickory chips. Cook 15 minutes per pound of fish.

When fillets are about half-done, place basil leaves, bay leaves and thyme under them and smoke until done. Baste often with butter and dry mustard mixture (Serves 4)

SIX WAYS to FRY FISH

1. Season generously with Tony's Creole Seasoning or salt and pepper, 2 cups corn meal and 1 cup flour. Place in paper bag. Make a slit lengthwise of perch or bite-size pieces of fillets. Add to corn meal mixture in paper bag and shake. Remove from bag, shake off excess mixture and drop in deep fat (375 degrees). Fry until brown and turn over once when they float. Remove and drain on absorbent paper.

2. For a change, spread mustard on fish before dipping in flour and meal mixture. Fry as directed above.

3. Soak in rich milk one hour. Drain, add to bag and shake. Remove and fry same way.

4. Soak fish in beer for 10 minutes before placing in paper bag. Fry as in No. 1.

5. The way I cook fish: cut slit lengthwise of perch and place in dishpan. Season all over generously with Tony's Creole Seasoning, and dash Worcestershire sauce and Louisiana Red Hot Sauce (mix all over fish inside and out). Dip in mixture of 2 cups corn meal, 1 cup flour—shake, fry in deep fat same way.

6. Instead of dipping in corn meal and flour, try pancake batter made by adding milk to soften. Dip seasoned fish and fry as directed in No. 1.

BAKED RED SNAPPER

4 pound red snapper
2 sticks margarine
1 cup chopped onions
1 cup chopped celery
½ cup chopped green bell pepper
4 cloves garlic, minced
1 teaspoon sugar
1 tablespoon Worcestershire sauce
¼ cup dry white wine
Tony's Creole Seasoning or salt and pepper
1 can tomato sauce

Season fish, inside and out, place in open baking pan. Make a sauce with margarine, tomato sauce, sugar and vegetables; cook over low heat for 1 hour. Pour wine over red snapper, followed by the sauce. Place in 300-degree oven; cook for 1 hour, basting occasionally. Serve with mashed Irish potatoes. (Serves 8)

NOTE: Stuff red snapper with crab meat and shrimp for a still better dish.

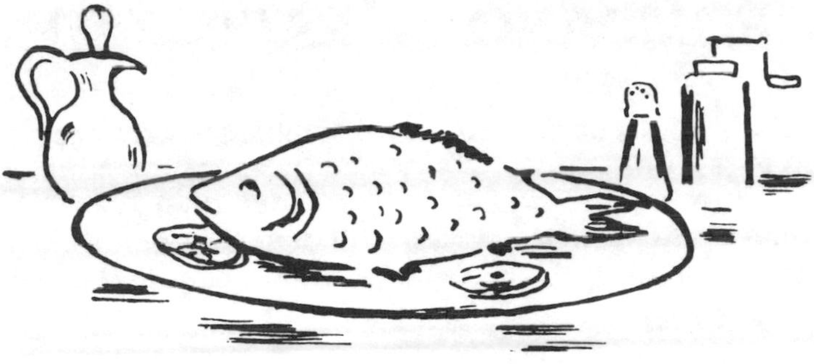

MUSHROOM-STUFFED BAKED RED SNAPPER

2 oven-ready whole red snappers, 2½ pounds each
½ cup dry white wine
¾ cup water
½ pound fresh mushrooms or
8-ounce can mushroom stems and pieces
3 tablespoons margarine, divided
½ cup finely chopped celery
5 tablespoons minced onions
8-ounce can water chestnuts, drained and finely chopped
½ cup soft bread crumbs
1 tablespoon chopped parsley
Tony's Creole Seasoning or salt and pepper

RINSE, pat dry and finely chop ¼ pound mushrooms. Quarter remaining mushrooms or drain canned mushrooms. Set aside.

In a small skillet melt 1 tablespoon margarine, add celery and 3 tablespoons of the onions. Saute 5 minutes. Combine sauted celery mixture with mushrooms, water chestnuts, bread crumbs, egg, soy sauce, parsley and seasoning. Mix well and spoon into fish cavity. Secure openings with skewer or toothpicks. Sprinkle both sides of the fish with Tony's Creole Seasoning.

Place in a large baking pan; dot with remaining 2 tablespoons of margarine, 2 tablespoons onion, the wine and water. Bake, uncovered, in a pre-heated moderate oven (350 degrees) 45 to 50 minutes. Baste occasionally. Test with a fork, when fish flakes it is done.

POMPANO en PAPILLOTE

4 medium-sized pompano
1 can mushroom soup
1 small can mushrooms
1 cup boiled, seasoned shrimp
½ sliced lemon
1 tablespoon chopped green onion tops (scallions)
1 pint water
Tony's Creole Seasoning to taste

Skin, clean and remove eyes, but leave head on. Place in a skillet with lemon slices and water. Poach for 5 minutes or until tender.

Make a thick sauce of mushroom soup, mushrooms, onion tops, boiled shrimp and Tony's Creole Seasoning. Simmer fish in sauce a few minutes. Then put fish and sauce in oiled paper bag or aluminum foil and place in oven in greased pan. Bake in moderate oven for 15 minutes. (Serves 4)

NOTE: Pompano may be broiled with butter and lime juice or barbecued. Cajuns believe pompano has the finest flavor of all fish.

FLOUNDER WITH SAUTERNE SAUCE

6 flounder fillets
½ cup sautern wine
6 small onion rings
2 tablespoons lemon juice
½ bay leaf
1 tablespoon margarine
tablespoon flour
2 egg yolks
¼ teaspoon salt
6 peppercorns

Place flounder fillets on onion rings in greased shallow baking dish. Add sauterne, lemon juice, bay leaf, salt and peppercorns, stir. Cover with a sheet of buttered wax paper. Bake in a moderate oven (350 degrees) for 15 minutes.

Remove fillets from baking dish and keep warm. Strain the sauce. Add water, if needed, to make 1 cup. Melt margarine, add flour and strained sauce. Cook, stirring constantly, until thickened. Beat egg yolks with 1 tablespoon of water and add to sauce, cook for 1 minute, stirring vigorously.

Place fillets in a shallow baking dish. Pour sauce over them. Set in a pan of boiling water in hot oven (400 degrees) for 3 minutes. Serve immediately. (Serves 6)

STUFFED FLOUNDER

2 medium-sized flounders, cleaned
½ pound fresh crab meat
7 slices bread
¼ cup butter
Small onion
Medium green bell pepper, chopped
1 cup diced celery
1 cup onion tops and bottoms, chopped
½ cup chopped parsley
Tony's Creole Seasoning or salt and pepper
Paprika
Juice of 1 lemon

Slit a pocket in the flounders to stuff. Start cutting by the fins and as close to bone as possible. Season inside and outside of fish with Tony's Creole Seasoning or salt and pepper.

Melt butter in skillet, add onions, bell pepper and celery; simmer until wilted. Soak bread in water, squeeze water from bread, break up in pieces and add to skillet. Add green onions, parsley, crab meat and seasoning. Cover skillet and cook on low heat about 15 minutes, stirring occasionally.

Fill flounder with bread stuffing, place in shallow buttered baking pan. Dot flounders with butter, pour lemon juice and bake in 350-degree oven for 40 to 45 minutes. Baste occasionally with drippings in pan. (Serves 2)

WALLEYED PERCH

Cooked a La Trout Meuniere

6 fillets of walleye
Tony's Creole Seasoning or salt and pepper
1 cup flour
1 pound butter
½ cup finely chopped parsley
1 lemon
Cream or milk

Season fillets with Tony's Seasoning or salt and pepper. Soak in cream or milk for 1 hour. Remove, dip in flour and fry in butter until brown. Turn over and brown the other side. Place fillets on hot serving dish and put slice of lemon on each fillet.

To pan juices add ½ cup finely chopped parsley and cook for 1 minute. Pour over the fillets and serve with French bread, green salad and Brabant potatoes. (Serves 6)

FILLET of SOLE MARGUERY

1½ pounds fillet of Sole or other fish
1 cup dry white wine
1 cup water
4 tablespoons or butter or margarine
4 tablespoons flour
1 cup milk
½ cup pure cream
1 tablespoon sherry
¼ teaspoon paprika
Salt and pepper to taste
12 small oysters
1 cup boiled, cooked shrimp

Heat dry white wine and water to boiling in a large skillet. Add fillet of Sole, cover and simmer very gently for 4 to 5 minutes or until fish is tender. Drain fish thoroughly. Reserve ½ cup of the liquid.

Melt butter and stir in flour. Add milk, cream and ½ cup of reserved fish liquid. Cook, stirring constantly until mixture is thick and smooth. Add sherry, paprika, salt and pepper.

Place fillets in a greased shallow baking dish or on an ovenproof platter. Arrange oysters and shrimp over fillets, cover with the sauce, and broil until bubbly and a delicate brown. (Serves 4)

TROUT MARGUERY

3 pounds tenderloin of trout
3 tablespoons olive oil
2 egg yolks, beaten
1 cup melted margarine
2 tablespoons lemon juice
1 cup cooked shrimp, chopped
½ cup cooked crab meat
½ cup sliced mushrooms
Paprika, salt and pepper to taste

Season fish in baking pan and add olive oil. Bake in 375-degree oven for 30 minutes. As fish bakes, prepare sauce.

To make sauce: place egg yolks in top of double boiler over hot, not boiling, water and gradually add melted margarine, stirring constantly until mixture thickens. Add lemon juice, shrimp, crab meat, mushrooms and seasoning to taste. Stir and cook for about 10 minutes to heat thoroughly.

Place baked fish on a platter and cover with sauce. (Serves 6)

TONY'S TROUT MEUNIERE

6 fillets, ½ pound each, bass or red snapper
1 cup rich milk
1 cup finely chopped parsley
1 cup flour
1 pound margarine
1 lemon
Tony's Creole Seasoning or salt and pepper

Season with Tony's Creole Seasoning or salt and pepper and cover with milk. Let stand in refrigerator for 1 hour. Dip in flour and fry in margarine 5 minutes on one side, and when brown, turn over and brown other side. Set cooked fillets in a serving dish. Garnish with slices of lemon.

Add 1 cup of finely chopped parsley to pan drippings and cook for 1 minute. Pour over the fillets and serve with small potatoes, green salad and French bread. (Serves 6)

TONY'S FISH COURTBOUILLON

6 to 8 pound fish, cut in pieces
1 cup flour
1 cup margarine
3 cups basic vegetable mixture (see page 5)
1 tablespoon Worcestershire sauce
½ lemon, sliced
Tony's Creole Seasoning
½ cup onion tops and parsley
1 small can tomato sauce
1 small can tomato paste
2 quarts water

In a Dutch oven, make a roux with flour and margarine. Cut off fire and add basic vegetable mix, stirring mixture until it stops sizzling. Add tomato paste and tomato sauce. Heat and stir over low heat for a few minutes. Add 2 quarts water, stir well and bring to boil. Add Worcestershire sauce and lemon slices. Lower heat, cover and let simmer at least 2 hours, stirring occasionally to prevent sticking on bottom.

Season with Tony's Creole Seasoning and add to mixture. Bring to boil, lower fire and simmer for 30 minutes to 1 hour. Add more water if too thick. Add onion tops and parsley and serve over boiled rice in soup bowl. (Serves 8)

TONY'S BOILED FISH with BIENVILLE SAUCE

6 fillets, about ½ pound each
Tony's Creole Seasoning or salt and pepper
3 cups Basic Cream Sauce (See page 7)
4-ounce can mushrooms
6 egg yolks
1 tablespoon grated onion
1 tablespoon minced parsley
¼ cup Parmesan cheese
½ teaspoon thyme
¼ cup dry white wine

Use bass, red snapper, speckled trout or any good white-fleshed fish.

Season fillets with Tony's Creole Seasoning and place in pot of hot water. Boil 5 minutes, remove and season again.

Place fillets in open baking dish. Make a Bienville Sauce, using 3 cups Basic Cream Sauce mixed with all other ingredients. Pour over the fish and bake in 300-degree oven for 10 minutes. (Serves 6)

BARBECUED FISH

6 pounds red snapper or bass
1 stick margarine
3 tablespoons grated onion
1 tablespoon grated green bell pepper
2 tablespoons minced parsley
2 tablespoons Worcestershire sauce
1 teaspoon Louisiana Red Hot sauce
2 lemons, sliced
Tony's Creole Seasoning or salt and pepper

Melt margarine in a saucepan. Add all other ingredients, except fish; stir well to mix. Place snapper on a sheet of heavy foil and pour sauce over fish. Seal foil making sure there is no leakage. Place on a grill, with a hood, if possible. Turn every 20 minutes, being careful not to tear the foil. Cook for 1½ hours. Remove from foil and place on grill for 10 minutes. Turn and cook another 10 minutes basting with sauce. (Serves 6)

TONY'S FISH SWAZELA

12 or 14 pieces of tenderloin fish, ½" thick and about 4 to 6 inches in diameter
1 can tomato paste
3 cans tomato sauce
6 large onions, sliced very thin
2 chopped green bell peppers
¼ stick chopped celery
1 cup dry white wine
4-ounce can mushrooms
½ cup green onion tops (scallions), chopped fine
½ lemon, sliced very thin
2 tablespoons Worcestershire sauce
1 cup salad oil

Saute onions in salad oil until well cooked. Add tomato paste, cook 5 minutes, stirring constantly. Add tomato sauce and cook 5 minutes. Add green bell peppers and celery, cook 15 minutes over very low fire. Add ½ cup wine, mushrooms, and cook 5 minutes. Add Worcestershire sauce, onion tops and sliced lemons. Let simmer and stir constantly. Use no water.

Season tenderloin fish with Tony's Creole Seasoning or salt and pepper. Put a layer of sauce ½ inch thick in bottom of Dutch oven, then a layer of fish, then a layer of sauce. Continue this until all fish is used. Cover with balance of sauce. Add another ½ cup wine, do not stir, cover tightly and let simmer 1 hour over very low fire. Do not stir, but turn the pot occasionally. Serve hot with crackers or rice. (Serves 6)

FISH CROQUETTES

2½ cups boiled, mashed potatoes
1 cup fish flakes
1 egg, well beaten
½ cup chopped green onion tops (scallions) and parsley
Tony's Creole Seasoning or salt and pepper
2 tablespoons flour
Deep fat for frying

Put potatoes through a ricer and beat well. Add egg, fish flakes, seasoning, onion tops and parsley. Mix thoroughly and shape into balls. Roll balls in flour and fry in deep fat until golden brown. (Serves 6)

SHERRY KETCHUP BAKED FISH

2 pounds of fillets, bass or other white-fleshed fish
Tony's Creole Seasoning or salt and pepper to taste
1 medium size onion, very thinly sliced
1 lemon, very thinly sliced
14-ounce bottle tomato ketchup
1/3 cup sherry
2 tablespoons melted margarine

Place fish on an oven-proof platter or in a shallow baking dish. Sprinkle with Tony's Creole Seasoning or salt and pepper to taste. Arrange onion and lemon slices on top. Mix ketchup, sherry and margarine; pour over fish. Bake in a moderately hot oven (375 degrees) for 50 minutes to 1 hour or until fish flakes when tested with a fork. (Serves 5 to 6)

JIM'S CHOUPIQUE, BAYOU COURTABLEAU STYLE

(Grinnell, mudfish, cypress trout, bowfin)

6 to 8 pound Choupique, skinned and filleted (must be caught in fresh water)
1/2 cup cooking oil
1 can Rotel tomatoes
1 can tomato sauce
4-ounce can mushrooms
1/2 sliced lemon
1 chopped green bell pepper
2 chopped onions
1/2 cup chopped onion tops
1/4 cup chopped parsley
8 chopped garlic cloves
Tony's Creole Seasoning to taste

Cut fish into small pieces. Season well and fry in cooking oil in Dutch oven. Fry until firm and remove from oil. To same oil add chopped onions, bell pepper and garlic and saute until brown. Then add tomato paste, tomato sauce, equal amount of water and fish to bring to a boil.

Lower heat and simmer for 45 minutes. Don't stir but shake pot occasionally. Add lemon slices, mushrooms, onion tops and parsley and cook over low heat for another 15 minutes. Serve with rice. (Serves 6 people)

TONY'S BLACKENED REDFISH

3 sticks unsalted butter, melted in a skillet
Tony's Creole Seasoning to taste
6-8 to 10 oz. fish fillets, cut ½ inch thick (redfish, salmon, red snapper, pompano)

Heat a large cast-iron skillet over very high heat until it is beyond the smoking stage, at least 10 minutes.

Meanwhile, dip each fillet in the melted butter so that both sides are well coated, then sprinkle Tony's Creole Seasoning generously and evenly on both sides of the fillet. Place in the hot skillet and pour one teaspoon melted butter on top of each fillet (watch carefully-butter may flame up). Cook, uncovered, over the same heat until the underside looks charred. ABOUT 2 minutes. Turn the fish over and again pour one teaspoon butter on top-cook until fish is done. Repeat with remaining fillets then serve while piping hot.

JIM BOWIE'S CREOLE GARFISH BOULETTES

3 pounds garfish meat
8 medium Irish potatoes
2 medium onions
1 egg
1 cup of mixed onion tops and parsley, chopped
2 cups all-purpose flour
Tony's Creole Seasoning or salt and pepper

Clean and skin garfish. With a fork scrape off meat so as to separate the gristle. Put onions and meat in a meat grinder. Mix with boiled mashed potatoes, onion tops and parsley, egg and season to taste Roll in 2-inch balls, dip in flour and fry in deep fat (375 degrees) until brown and floating. They go good in Court-bouillon or serve as is.

RAW FISH SEVICHE

1 pound raw fish fillets, snook, red snapper or any white-fleshed salt water fish
1 large ripe tomato, peeled and sliced
1 large onion, thinly sliced
10 Mexican hot chili peppers or Louisiana red hot peppers, chopped
1 teaspoon coriander seeds
1 cup tomato juice
2 cups lime juice (fresh limes)
6 tablespoons olive oil
¼ teaspoon oregano
¼ cup dry white wine
Salt to taste
Onion slices for garnish
Crackers

Cut fillets into bite-size pieces. Put fish in a serving dish and cover with sliced tomato, onion, peppers, coriander seed, tomato juice, olive oil, wine, lime juice, oregano and salt to taste. Stir lightly and marinate the fish in a refrigerator overnight. Serve chilled, garnished with thinly-sliced onions on crackers.

TONY'S CRAWFISH SUPREME

½ lb. crawfish tails (uncooked)
1 package frozen chopped spinach
1 stick butter or margarine
3 tablespoons all purpose flour
2 cups of milk or half and half
4 egg yolks, slightly beaten
½ medium onion, minced
1 2-ounce can sliced mushrooms
2 tablespoons chopped parsley
¼ cup grated Parmesan cheese
Tony's Chachere's Famous Creole Seasoning to taste

Season crawfish tails with Tony's Seasoning and saute crawfish in ¼ stick butter for 5 minutes. Remove crawfish and set aside. Add balance of butter and 3 tablespoons flour. Stir until smooth. Gradually add milk and cook until thick, stirring constantly. Carefully add egg yolks and cook to boiling point, but do not boil. Remove from heat and check seasoning to taste. Stir in parsley, onions, and mushrooms.Cook spinach as directed on package. Place a layer of cooked spinach in bottom of buttered casserole. Add a layer of crawfish and pour sauce over crawfish. Sprinkle with Parmesan Cheese on top of casserole. Bake at 375 degrees for about 10 minutes. (Serves 4)

TONY'S CHICKEN and SAUSAGE JAMBALAYA

1 large fryer, cut up
½ lb. smoked pork sausage
1 stick margarine
3 cups uncooked rice
4 large onions, chopped
4 cloves garlic, minced
2 sticks celery, chopped
1 bell pepper, chopped
Tony Chachere's Famous Creole Seasoning to taste

Season cut up chicken generously with Tony Chachere's Famous Creole Seasoning. Add margarine to 5 quart Dutch oven and fry chicken until brown. Add all vegetables and saute for 10 minutes. Add sausage and rice and cook for 10 minutes mixing as you go. Add 4 cups water, stir well and cover until rice is fully cooked. Keep covered. (Serves 8)

GAME

TONY'S ALLIGATOR SAUCE PIQUANTE

3 pounds alligator meat cut in pieces
3 cups Tony's Basic Vegetables Mix (see page 5)
1 can Rotel tomatoes
1 cup burgundy wine
1 6 oz. can tomato sauce
¼ cup Tony's Creole Roux & Gravy Mix
Enough water to cover meat
2 tablespoons Worcestershire sauce
Tony's Famous Creole Seasoning (enough)
2 sticks butter or oleo
½ teaspoon sugar

Season meat generously with Tony Chachere's Famous Creole Seasoning. Fry in melted butter or oleo. Add Basic Vegetable Mix, cook for about 5 minutes until vegetables are soft. Add tomato paste and Rotel tomatoes with ½ teaspoon sugar, cook another 5 minutes while stirring. Mix a ¼ cup of Creole Roux to enough water to cover meat, add to mixture. Add all other ingredients, let come to a boil, then let simmer for 3 to 4 hours until meat is tender and water is cooked down and gravy is just right. Season again to taste with Tony Chachere's Famous Creole Seasoning and serve with boiled rice.

BRICE PALMER'S FRIED ALLIGATOR

3 pounds of boneless alligator meat (cut into one-inch cubes)
3 cups of milk or evaporated milk
1 cup of mustard
2 tablespoons of Tony's Creole Seasoning
2 cups fish fry mix
2 cups pancake mix
Cooking oil for frying

Cut the alligator into one-inch cubes and then soak meat in milk (in refrigerator) for 2 to 3 hours. Drain milk then season meat (in same bowl) with Tony's Creole Seasoning. Add mustard and mix well. Mix fish fry and pancake mix in shaking bag. Drop meat cubes in shaking bag and coat well. Deep fry at 375 degrees for 5-6 minutes or until golden brown. Serve hot with French fries and seafood sauce.

TONY'S BARBECUED ALLIGATOR TAIL

Cut tail into 1" thick slices like steak. Season generously with Tony Chachere's Famous Creole Seasoning. Place on Pit and dab with Tony Chachere's Creole Barbecue Sauce to which has been added 1 stick margarine to each pint of sauce. Serve with the sauce. It's great.

ROAST GOOSE with SAUERKRAUT and BREAD DUMPLINGS

8 to 10 pound goose
1 cup water
4 pounds fresh, canned or packaged sauerkraut
2 cups finely chopped onions
1 cup grated raw potato
2 cups finely chopped apples
1 tablespoon caraway seed
Freshly ground black pepper
Salt to taste

Preheat oven to 325 degrees. Remove all loose fat from inside goose and dice fat into ½ inch chunks. In a small covered saucepan simmer fat with a cup of water, for 20 minutes. Uncover pan and boil liquid completely away. Fat will begin to sputter. Continue to cook until it stops. Strain fat into a bowl and reserve.

Drain sauerkraut and wash well under cold running water. To reduce sourness, soak it in cold water about 20 minutes. Squeeze dry by the handful. Heat 6 tablespoons of goose fat in a heavy 12-inch skillet and add onions and sauerkraut. Stirring occasionally, cook uncovered about 10 minutes. Transfer sauerkraut mixture to a large mixing bowl. Add apples, potato, ½ teaspoon salt, caraway seeds and a few grindings of pepper.

Wash goose inside and out with cold running water. Pat dry with paper towels and sprinkle cavity generously with salt and a few grindings of pepper. Fill goose with sauerkraut stuffing, sew up opening and truss legs with cord. Set goose breast up on a rack in a large roasting pan. Cook in oven 2 to 3 hours, or 25 minutes to the pound.

Remove excess grease with a bulb baster. Goose is done when juice from punctured thigh runs pale yellow. When done, remove goose to serving platter and cut away thread and cord. Transfer stuffing to a serving dish, garnish with strips of parsley and surround with bread dumplings (see page 164). Let goose set for 15 minutes before carving. (Serves 6 to 8)

JIM BOWIE'S CLAY-BAKED DUCK

1 goose
1 mallard duck
Tony's Creole Seasoning or salt and pepper
½ onion
1 stick celery

Clay-baking is one way Jim Bowie had of enjoying the delectable taste of duck. First, kill a goose. Do not remove feathers. Goose must first be drawn, but feathers may be left on. Then kill a mallard duck. Clean and dress duck. Season duck with Tony's Creole Seasoning or salt, black pepper and red pepper. Place ½ onion and 1 stalk celery inside duck.

Place duck inside goose. Roll out a sheet of moistened clay mud and wrap goose in it. Place in a bed of hickory coals and cover with coals. Bake 3 to 4 hours, then remove duck from goose. Juices of the goose tenderize and flavor the mallard. Eat the duck and throw goose away.

In the day of Jim Bowie, old blue goose and snow goose were considered too tough to eat. They only ate the delectable ring neck.

COOT in SOY SAUCE

2 coots (poule d'eau)
4 teaspoons soy sauce
¼ cup lime juice
¼ teaspoon salt
Small pieces of ginger root
6 water chestnuts, sliced
2 pieces celery

Skin and parboil two coots. Remove breasts and marinate in a mixture of soy sauce, lime juice, dash of salt and several slivers of ginger. Let soak for several hours. Drain and broil for 30 minutes, basting with marinade and melted butter. Add slices of water chestnuts and when almost done, garnish with slices of celery. (Serves 2)

NOTE: Coot breasts and gizzards make an excellent gumbo.

WILD DUCKS a la GEORGE BROUSSARD

(with Black Iron Pot on top of stove)

4 whole ducks, dressed
4 onions
4 sticks celery
1 bell pepper
2 cans chicken broth
1 cup Burgundy wine
1 cup onion tops, and parsley, mixed and chopped
8-ounce can mushrooms
Tony's Creole Seasoning
1 cup bacon drippings

Season duck inside and out generously with Tony's Creole Seasoning. Chop vegetables, mix and add equally to inside of each duck.

Place duck in black Dutch oven on top of stove, add bacon drippings and brown ducks all over. Add wine, chicken broth and enough water to cover ducks. Bring to boil. Cut fire to simmer and cook until tender. Then remove from pot and add onion tops, parsley, mushrooms, and mushroom juice thickened with a little flour. Cook five minutes. Add water if more gravy is needed. It takes 3 to 4 hours to completely cook. (Serves 8)

BAKED TEAL with OYSTERS

6 teal, dressed and drawn
1½ dozen fresh oysters
½ onion grated
½ cup Burgundy wine
2 strips bacon
1 stick margarine
½ cup onion tops and parsley
1 small can mushrooms
2 tablespoons currant jelly
1 can chicken bouillon
1 tablespoon flour
Tony's Creole Seasoning or salt and pepper

You can do the same with mallards, pintails or other ducks.

Season teal inside and out with Tony's Creole Seasoning. Stuff 3 oysters in each duck with slice of margarine and teaspoonful grated onion. Skewer with toothpicks and thread.

Melt ½ stick margarine in covered baking dish. Place teals, breast side up, add two strips bacon on top and rest of sliced margarine. Cook until brown in 450-degree oven with top off the pan. Add bouillon and wine. Reduce heat to 300 degrees, cover and cook about 2 hours. Turn over on breast when about half done. When tender enough to remove breast bone, take out, add onion tops, parsley, mushrooms and currant jelly to the pan juice. Mix mushroom juice with tablespoon of flour and add to gravy. Place on top of stove and cook for 5 minutes until thickened. Try mallards, or pintail, same way. (Serves 6)

MEXICAN FRIED DOVE

10 white wing doves
1 egg
1 cup milk
2 cups pancake flour
Tony's Creole Seasoning or salt and pepper

Clean doves, singe, split down the back and flatten. Season with Tony's Creole Seasoning or salt and pepper. Soak in mixture of milk and egg. When ready to fry, dip in pancake flour and drop in deep fat, 375 degrees. When doves float to the top and brown, remove and drain on absorbent paper. The secret of tender dove is quick frying. Takes about 10 minutes to brown.

NOTE: I know a fellow who ate 15 doves at one sitting! You can cook quail, grouse, snipe or woodcock the same way. The Cajun likes his fried dove for breakfast.

SHERRIED DOVES

4 doves dressed
½ cup flour
1 stick butter
1 cup chopped green onion tops
4 ripe tomatoes
½ green bell pepper
1 hot red pepper
Tony's Creole Seasoning or salt and pepper
1 clove garlic
3 cups chicken stock (or bouillon)
1 cup sherry wine

Season birds with Tony's Creole Seasoning or salt and pepper. Roll in flour and fry in butter for 20 minutes. In another skillet saute chopped vegetables for 10 minutes. Add chicken stock and doves and simmer for 1 hour. Add 1 cup sherry and simmer another 30 minutes. Serve with boiled rice. (Serves 4)

SMOTHERED DOVES ACADIENNE

8 doves, cleaned and singed
2 onions, chopped
1 bell pepper, chopped
2 sticks celery, chopped
1 tablespoon parsley, chopped
2 tablespoons chopped onion tops (scallions)
4 cloves garlic, chopped fine
4-ounce can mushrooms
2 sticks margarine
1 tablespoon Worcestershire sauce
1 tablespoon flour
1 cup Burgundy wine
Tony's Creole Seasoning or salt and pepper

Melt margarine in Dutch oven, add doves and cook until brown, stirring constantly until they begin to stick at the bottom. Then add onions, celery, bell pepper, garlic and Worcestershire sauce. Cook until wilted. Add Burgundy, cover and simmer for 2 to 3 hours until birds are tender. As you know, doves are tough and need a long time to cook. Add 4 ounces cold water if needed.

When doves are tender, remove from the pan liquid. Add mushrooms, mixture of flour blended with the mushroom juice, onion tops and parsley. If you like a sweet gravy, add 2 tablespoons currant jelly. Serve with spaghetti or boiled rice. (Serves 8)

NOTE: Cook snipe, woodcock or grouse the same way.

DOVE CASSEROLE

6 doves
6 small onions
6 tablespoons chopped parsley
½ cup butter
1 garlic clove, minced
2½ cups canned tomatoes
6-ounce can mushrooms
1 large onion, chopped
½ teaspoon thyme
¼ teaspoon dried basil
1 teaspoon salt
Freshly ground black pepper

Stuff each dove with one onion, 1 tablespoon parsley and 1 teaspoon butter. Saute garlic in remaining 6 tablespoons butter for 5 minutes. Add doves and saute for 10 minutes or until brown on all sides. Put doves and garlic butter in a deep casserole and add remaining ingredients. Cover and bake in a moderate oven (375 degrees) until done, about 2 hours. Serve on a platter. (Serves 6)

TONY'S QUAIL RECIPE

6 quail
1 tablespoon chopped onions
1 tablespoon chopped celery
1 tablespoon chopped green bell pepper
1 stick butter or margarine
1 strip bacon
1 cup chicken bouillon
1 tablespoon sherry wine
4-ounce can mushrooms
1 tablespoon flour
Tony's Creole Seasoning or salt and pepper

In a Dutch oven, melt butter and fry seasoned quail until brown. Remove birds, stuff each cavity with mixture (teaspoonful) of chopped vegetables. Replace in pot and add bouillon soup, wine and all other ingredients, except mushrooms and flour. Cover, place in 300-degree oven and cook 1 hour until tender. Remove quail, add mushrooms and a little flour to thicken. One tablespoon currant jelly goes good in the gravy. (Serves 6)

QUAIL en CASSEROLE

6 quail
3 slices bread, slightly toasted
½ teaspoon savory
Salt and pepper
3 strips bacon
⅓ cup water
2 teaspoons butter

Clean and remove skin from quail. Rub each with salt and butter. Roll slightly toasted bread into small pieces. Add pepper, salt, savory, butter. Stuff birds and wrap each with ½ strip bacon. Place in casserole with pat of butter, and ⅓ cup water. Cover and cook in oven until tender.

MEXICAN BAKED QUAIL

2 quail, cut up in pieces
1 cup cream
2 tablespoons olive oil
Salt and pepper to taste
¼ teaspoon grated nutmeg
4-ounce can mushrooms stems and pieces
Guava jelly

Soak 2 disjointed quail overnight in cream, salt and pepper. Dry and brown evenly in olive oil. Sprinkle with grated nutmeg. Place in a casserole with sliced mushrooms and some of the mushroom juice. Bake 2 hours in a moderate oven. Serve hot with rice and guava jelly. (Serves 2)

QUAIL SAUTEED in WILD GAME SAUCE

6 quail, split down the back
6 medium buns
¾ cup butter
Tony's Creole Seasoning or salt and pepper
2½ cups Wild Game Sauce **(See page 13)**

Saute quail over high heat in ½ cup butter for 10 minutes or until golden brown. Sprinkle with Tony's Creole Seasoning or salt and pepper. Split buns in half and hollow out centers. Toast in a low oven (325 degrees) until brown. Melt ¼ cup butter and brush buns with butter. Arrange quail on buns and serve with Wild Game Sauce. (Serves 6)

CREAMED SNIPE

10 snipe
1 medium onion, grated
1 tablespoon salt
1 tablespoon freshly ground black pepper
½ teaspoon thyme
½ cup chicken stock
½ cup sherry
2 tablespoons brandy
1 cup heavy cream
½ cup butter
parsley
lemon slices

Dry snipe inside and out with paper towels. Combine salt, black pepper and thyme. Rub seasoning inside and out of snipe. Saute snipe in butter until brown and remove to covered casserole. Add onions and chicken stock to butter in frying pan. Cut fire, add sherry over snipe. Cover casserole, bake in 350-degree oven until done.

Remove snipe, finish sauce with cream, heat until thickened a little (do not boil), add brandy and pour sauce over birds. Serve hot on platter. Garnish with parsley and slices of lemon. (Serves 10)

BROILED BRANDIED SNIPE

4 snipe, dressed and drawn
1 tablespoon Worcestershire sauce
¼ cup lemon juice
1 stick butter or margarine
Brandy
Tony's Creole Seasoning or salt and pepper

Season snipe, brush with melted butter and baste with mixture of lemon juice, Worcestershire sauce and butter. Broil until well-browned and tender (about 30 minutes). Pour brandy over birds, flame and serve. (Serves 2 to 4)

SMOTHERED SNIPE

5 snipe, dressed
½ cup vermouth (dry)
½ cup olive oil
½ cup flour
1 stick butter or margarine
1 can chicken bouillon soup (or stock)
½ cup sherry
Tony's Creole Seasoning or salt and pepper to taste

Marinate snipe in mixture of olive oil and vermouth for 1 hour. Dry and season birds well inside and out. Sprinkle with flour, brown in butter for 10 minutes. Add chicken bouillon and simmer for 1 hour. Add sherry and cook another 10 minutes. (Serves 3 to 6)

TRY TONY CHACHERE'S SALT FREE CREOLE SEASONING

At last relief for those of you who enjoy good cooking, but cannot use salt.

Tastes like salt plus the wonderful spices, but contains no salt. It's an exact blend of our Tony Chachere's Famous Creole Seasoning without the salt. Contains a salt alternative. No bitter taste.

GROUSE in WHITE WINE

4 grouse
Chopped livers, gizzards and hearts of grouse
1 stick butter
1 cup dry white wine
1 tablespoon chopped parsley
3 tablespoons chopped scallions
2 whole cloves
4-ounce can mushrooms
Tony's Creole Seasoning or salt and pepper

Clean and singe grouse then split in halves. Melt butter in large skillet or Dutch oven. Season grouse and brown in butter. Add chopped scallions, livers, gizzards, hearts and ½ cup wine. Reduce heat, cover the skillet and let simmer gently for 15 minutes. Add parsley, another ½ cup wine, cloves and mushrooms. Cook for 15 minutes or until tender. (Serves 4)

GROUSE with ORANGE SLICES

4 grouse
Tony's Creole Seasoning or salt and pepper to taste
4 slices bacon
4 quarter-inch thick orange slices peeled and seeded
¼ cup margarine, melted
1 orange peel, grated
2 tablespoons orange juice
1 tablespoon lemon juice
Chopped parsley

Sprinkle grouse inside and out with Tony's Creole Seasoning or salt and pepper to taste. Cover breast of each with orange slice and a bacon slice, fastened with toothpicks.

Place grouse breast up in a baking pan. Roast in a preheated 350-degree oven 15 to 20 minutes or until tender.

Baste frequently with combined margarine, orange peel, orange juice and lemon juice. Remove toothpicks and sprinkle with parsley. Serve with roasted orange and bacon slices, boiled rice, green peas and a green salad. (Serves 4)

NOTE: The rich, dark meat needs only a brief cooking and is best when broiled or roasted. The birds are about the size of a small chicken.

ROAST GROUSE with WINE SAUCE

6 grouse
¾ cup dry red wine
Celery leaves
12 slices bacon
1 tablespoon butter
1 tablespoon minced onion
¾ cup beef bouillon
1 teaspoon salt
Freshly ground black pepper

Rub grouse cavities with salt and pepper. Stuff each grouse with celery leaves and 1 teaspoon butter. Cover breasts with bacon slices and roast in moderate oven (375 degrees) for 1 hour. Remove grouse and keep hot.

In pan juices saute onion over low heat for 5 minutes or until onion turns golden brown. Add wine and bouillon. Bring to a boil and cook 5 minutes, stirring and scraping the pan. Serve sauce with grouse. (Serves 6)

ROAST PHEASANT with CREAM and BRANDY

pheasants, cleaned
2 cups heavy cream
2 cups chicken bouillon
½ cup brandy
1 onion, thinly sliced
¼ cup butter
6 slices bacon
¼ cup horseradish
1 teaspoon salt
Freshly ground black pepper

Saute onion in butter in a roasting pan for 5 minutes. Add pheasants and saute over high heat for 15 minutes or until brown on all sides. Pour some brandy into a ladle and the rest over the pheasants. Warm ladle over a match, light the brandy and flame the pheasants. When flame dies, add bouillon, salt and pepper.

Put bacon over pheasants breasts and roast uncovered in 375-degree oven for 45 minutes, basting frequently. Stir cream and horseradish into pan juices and continue roasting 15 minutes, basting frequently. Serve pheasant and sauce with boiled rice. (Serves 6)

LOUISIANA CAJUN'S SQUIRREL STEW

(--The one and only)

4 squirrels, cut in pieces including the heads
1 stick margarine
1 cup chopped onions
½ cup chopped green bell pepper
4 cloves garlic
1 tablespoon Worcestershire sauce
½ cup Burgundy wine
1 tablespoon chopped green onion tops
1 tablespoon chopped parsley
4-ounce can mushrooms
1 tablespoon flour
Tony's Creole Seasoning or salt and pepper

Cut each squirrel into eight pieces, including the heads. Season with Tony's Creole Seasoning or salt and pepper. Melt margarine in a Dutch oven and fry squirrels until browned all over until they start to stick in the pot. Add a cup of chopped onions, ½ cup of bell peppers and 4 cloves garlic.

When vegetables are soft, add a small amount of cold water, a tablespoon of Worcestershire sauce, cover the pot and let simmer about 1 hour. Stir well and add ½ cup burgundy wine. Cook until tender.

Remove the squirrels from the pot and add to the remaining juices a tablespoon of flour mixed with liquid from can of mushrooms. Add mixture of a tablespoon of chopped onion tops, tablespoon of finely chopped parsley and the mushrooms. Cook for 5 minutes, stirring until slightly thickened and pour over squirrel.

Serve with boiled rice or spaghetti. (Serves 8)

BAKED JUICY SWAMP RABBIT

3 pounds dressed rabbit, cut in pieces
1 stick margarine
1 cup flour
1 onion chopped
1 bell pepper
2 sticks celery
4 cloves garlic
1 tablespoon Worcestershire sauce
1 can tomato paste
Tony's Creole Seasoning or salt and pepper
Water

Season rabbit well with Tony's Creole Seasoning or salt and pepper. Dip in flour and fry in margarine until brown. Add finely chopped onion, bell pepper, celery and garlic. Cook until tender. Add Worcestershire sauce, tomato paste and enough water to cook rabbit until tender and still have a nice thick gravy. (Serves 4)

ROAST RABBIT

1 rabbit, dressed
½ cup ground pork
½ cup ground beef
1 cup bread crumbs
1 egg, beaten
1 onion, chopped
1 carrot, chopped
1 sprig parsley, chopped
4 cloves
1 sprig thyme, crushed
1 bay leaf, crushed
½ cup white wine
Tony's Creole Seasoning or salt and pepper
1 cup hot water
1 cup milk
1 stick margarine, melted
1 tablespoon flour

Wash rabbit and soak in slightly salted water for 1 hour or longer. Dry, rub well with Tony's Creole Seasoning or salt and pepper. Stuff with a dressing prepared from the bread crumbs, ground meat mixed with egg, and seasoning. Skewer. Sift flour over top of rabbit and place in roasting pan on a bed of chopped onion, carrot, parsley, crushed thyme, bay leaf and the cloves. Moisten with hot water.

Cover and roast in 300-degree oven, basting frequently, for 2 hours, first with milk until half-done and then with melted margarine. Before serving add wine to gravy and pour over rabbit. (Serves 4)

NOTE: Serve with wine and currant jelly.

ROAST VENISON

Hind quarter of venison (about 10 pounds)
1 chopped green bell pepper
1 chopped onion
2 sticks celery, chopped
4 cloves garlic, minced
2 sticks margarine
4 strips bacon
8-ounce can mushrooms
Tony's Creole Seasoning or salt and pepper
1 cup Burgundy wine
1 tablespoon minced green onions (scallions)
1 tablespoon parsley, minced

Cut a pocket along the leg bone from the large end almost to small end. Season the roast well inside pocket and rub well outside. Fill pocket with all the chopped vegetables except onion tops, parsley and mushrooms. Pour wine over roast and add 4 strips bacon on top.

Place in covered roasting pan and cook in 300 degree oven for 3 to 4 hours until tender. Remove from pan, add tablespoon of flour to juice from mushrooms and mix well. Add, along with mushrooms, onion tops and parsley to pan juices. Place over high heat and cook 5 minutes until gravy thickens. Put roast back into gravy and cook, uncovered, for 5 minutes to brown. Slice and serve ½ pound per person.

If you like your gravy sweet, add 2 tablespoons currant jelly.

TASTY VENISON CHOPS

4 large shoulder venison chops
2 tablespoons vegetable oil
1 cup honey
1 cup dry white wine
2 tablespoons Worcestershire
1 large garlic clove, crushed
½ teaspoon powdered ginger
Few drops Tabasco sauce

Brown chops slowly on both sides in oil. Combine remaining ingredients, mix well, pour over chops. Simmer over very low heat about 45 minutes or until tender. Serve chops and sauce over hot, buttered macaroni. (Serves 4)

BREADED VENISON SCHNITZEL

2 pounds leg of venison, cut into slices 1/4 inch thick
1 cup fresh lemon juice
Salt
Freshly ground black pepper
2 eggs
1/4 cup flour
2 tablespoons water
1 cup fine bread crumbs
1 1/2 cups shortening

In a glass baking dish marinate the cutlets in lemon juice for 1 hour. Pat them dry with a paper towel and sprinkle with salt and pepper. Dip in eggs beaten with water, then dip in flour, shake off the excess, and finally dip them in bread crumbs. Gently shake off any excess bread crumbs and refrigerate for at least 1/2 hour.

Heat shortening in a heavy 12-inch skillet until hot, then add cutlets. Cook over medium heat 3 or 4 minutes on each side or until golden brown. Use tongs to turn them. Garnish with lemon wedges and serve immediately. (Serves 4)

VENISON PARMESAN

1 pound thin venison steak (1/4" thick)
Salt and pepper
1 egg
1/3 cup grated Parmesan cheese
1/3 cup fine dried bread crumbs
1/4 cup olive oil
2 tablespoons butter
1 onion, finely chopped
6-ounce can tomato paste
2 cups hot water
1 teaspoon salt
1/2 teaspoon marjoram
1/2 pound Mozzarella or Swiss cheese

Cut steaks into 6 or 8 pieces, sprinkle with salt and pepper. Beat egg with 2 teaspoons of water. Dip meat in egg, then roll in mixture of cheese and crumbs. Heat oil in large skillet and fry the pieces (about 3 at a time) until golden brown on each side. Lay in shallow, wide baking dish.

In same skillet cook onions in butter until soft. Add tomato paste mixed with hot water, salt, and marjoram. Boil a few minutes, scraping all of the brown bits from the bottom. Pour most of the sauce over steaks. Top with thin slices of cheese, then pour over remaining sauce. Bake in moderate oven, 350 degrees, for about 30 minutes. (Serves 4)

VENISON DAUBE GLACE

10 pounds hindquarter of venison
1½ cups juice from pickled hot peppers
¼ cup cooking oil
6 small medium onions, quartered
2 sticks celery with tops
6 carrots, halved
4 bay leaves
Pinch of thyme
4 ounces sherry
3 packs gelatin, unflavored
4 hard-boiled eggs, sliced
2 lemons, sliced
½ pint pure cream with horseradish to taste
1 dozen cloves
Salt to taste

Put daube in pan and pour pepper vinegar over it. Salt to taste and allow to soak overnight or up to 24 hours, turning once. Drain the meat (retaining marinade) and brown in cooking oil in large pot. Cover with water. Add the onions, carrots, celery, bay leaf, thyme, cloves, black pepper, cayenne and vinegar marinade. Simmer on top of stove 4 to 5 hours or until meat is tender. Remove meat, strain liquid and reserve.

Three pints of liquid are necessary for a 10 pound roast. If too much, reduce by boiling down, if too little add water, then add sherry. Bring to a boil and add gelatin, presoftened in small amount of water. Taste for correct seasoning of salt and red pepper.

Remove all fat, bone and tendons from meat and break into chunk-size pieces. Meat should be so tender that knife is hardly necessary.

In bottom of large mold or vegetable crisper or refrigerator (which is right size), arrange sliced hard-boiled eggs and lemon slices. Place meat evenly over surface. Pour liquid gently over whole and jell in the refrigerator. Any grease in liquid will rise to top and can be easily removed when firm.

Turn mold over onto large platter and decorate with parsley and other greens. Serve with horseradish sauce in a side dish.

NOTE: Any good beef roast can also be used.

CREAMED VENISON CHOPS

4 venison chops
¾ cup cream
Tony's Creole Seasoning or salt and pepper
2 tablespoons olive oil
½ cup flour
Cooking oil for frying

Marinate chops overnight in cream, Tony's Creole Seasoning or salt and pepper. Wipe dry and rub with olive oil. Dust with flour and fry for 30 minutes or until done. Serve with Yankee Cream Gravy and boiled rice. (Serves 4)

BAKED COON and SWEET POTATOES

1 skinned and dressed whole coon
1 cup red wine
1 onion, chopped
2 strips bacon
1 green bell pepper, chopped
2 sticks celery, chopped
4 cloves garlic
2 sticks margarine
1 tablespoon Worcestershire sauce
Tony's Creole Seasoning or salt and pepper
6 medium-size sweet potatoes, peeled

Boil coon for 1 hour to tenderize. Remove, dry and season with Tony's Creole Seasoning or salt and pepper. Sink holes, 2 on each side, and fill with garlic cloves. Place chopped vegetables and 1 stick margarine inside cavity. Place in a greased roasting pan and cover with bacon.

Pour wine over coon, arrange sweet potatoes around sides and 1 stick margarine to pan. Bake in open pan at 300 degrees, basting often, until tender. Serve with sweet potatoes and boiled rice. (Serves 8)

The armadillo made a mistake when he crossed the Sabine River into Louisiana. The Cajuns in Louisiana are fast learning of the delectable taste of this animal and you can bet your boots he will be trying to get back to Texas before too long.

CLEVE'S SMOTHERED ARMADILLO

Prepare an armadillo by placing on its back, cut off head, tail and feet. Remove belly skin. Then pass the knife along and around shell and remove it. Then clean same as you would a turtle. Wash, then scald the meat. Remove all excess fat. Cut up in pieces.

3 pounds meat
2 chopped onions
1 chopped bell pepper
2 cloves garlic, minced
2 sticks celery, chopped
1 stick margarine
½ cup mixed onion tops and parsley, chopped
1 tablespoon flour
1 tablespoon Worcestershire sauce
Small can of mushrooms
½ cup Burgundy wine
Tony's Creole Seasoning or salt and pepper

Add margarine to a Dutch oven. Fry meat until brown. Add all the vegetables and let saute 5 minutes. Add the wine and mushroom juice. Cover the pot and let simmer until meat is tender, add water if needed. Remove meat from pot and add to the juices a mixture of water and flour to make a smooth paste. Also add at this time, the onion tops and parsley, mushrooms and enough water necessary to make a gravy. Cook 5 minutes and pour over the meat and serve with white rice. (Serves 6)

NOTE: Barbecued armadillo is very good. Cut in pieces and marinate meat over night. Still better!

The recipe above was given to me by Cleveland DeVillier, age 79. He still hunts, fishes and cooks. He and his wonderful wife reared 13 children, 12 of whom are still living. One son was lost in Korea. He put all of them through college while working 80 acres as a share cropper. He and his 12-year-old son used to cut as much as 3 ranks of wood per day at 75 cents per rank to keep his family going. Some man! Backbone of America! I'm proud to be his friend.

TONY'S NUTRIA SAUCE PIQUANTE

4 pounds dressed Nutria (cut in pieces)
1 stick margarine
2 tablespoons flour
3 cups Basic Vegetable Mix (See page 5)
1 cup Burgundy wine
1 tablespoon Worcestershire sauce
4-ounce can mushrooms
1 cup water
Tony's Famous Creole Seasoning to taste

Season nutria pieces generously with Tony's Famous Creole Seasoning. Melt margarine in Dutch oven and fry nutria, stirring constantly until meat starts to stick to bottom. Add Basic Vegetable mix and saute 5 to 10 minutes. Add Burgundy wine and Worcestershire sauce, stir and bring to boil. Reduce heat, cover and simmer about 2 hours or until tender. Stir occasionally.

Make a mixture of flour and 1 cup water. Add to pot with the mushrooms and mushroom liquid. Stir until a thick gravy is made, about 5 minutes.

NOTE: Cajun hunters and trappers have long known what nutritionists are just beginning to publicize — that nutria meat is of high-quality, is taste-tempting and has much to offer pennywise. The nutria is a beaver-like aquatic animal which eats only vegetation and is renowned for its fur. It was brought to Avery Island, Louisiana in 1930 from South America for experimental breeding stock. A hurricane in 1940 scattered the penned animals into the marshland. Being prolific breeders they soon "took over" the Louisiana marshlands and now provide 95 percent of the world's supply of nutria fur and meat.

See order blanks
in back of book.

MEATS AND POULTRY

TONY CHACHERE'S CREOLE CRAB BOIL 9 oz.

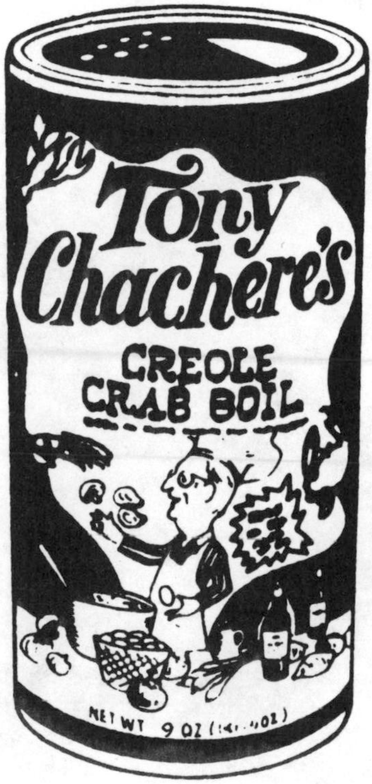

Contains salt,
red pepper,
and other spices,
garlic,
onions and
lemon.

"Ready to use, nothing to add".

CHARCOAL RIBEYE STEAK

Good steaks are a man's job! From time to time your local supermarket has on sale prime or U.S. Choice rib racks of heavy beef. Have the butcher select a choice rack, about 35 lbs. He will be happy to let it hang in his freezer for 21 days to age it. Then have him cut it into ribeye steaks, 1 inch thick. Have him wrap them 1 to a package for your freezer. You will get 16, plus 5- or 6-pound rack of ribs to barbecue and 2 pounds of meat cut in chunks for skewering.

If you haven't tried to buy your steaks this way you have been missing something. Season steaks with Tony's Creole Seasoning or salt and pepper. Place on charcoal broiler, baste with mixture of lemom juice, 1 stick margarine, 1 tablespoon Worcestershire sauce. When pink in the middle, serve. They'll melt in your mouth.

CREOLE BAKED TONGUE

1 beef tongue, cleaned
1 cup cooking oil
1 carrot, length of tongue
1 small bell pepper, chopped
6 cloves garlic, minced
Tony's Creole Seasoning or salt and pepper
1 small onion, chopped

Cut slit length of tongue. Season with Tony's Creole Seasoning or salt and pepper and stuff with chopped vegetables. Place carrot length-wise in opening and sew up.

In Dutch oven, fry tongue in oil until brown, adding ice cold water as needed to keep from burning and also to make gravy brown. Continue cooking, about 2 hours adding cold water as needed, and turning. When tender, slice crosswise and serve with gravy on rice. (Serves 4)

MARINATED PORK GRILLADES

1 pound pork steaks
2 tablespoons chopped onion
½ cup vinegar
¼ stick margarine
Tony's Creole Seasoning or salt and black pepper

Cut steaks in 2-inch pieces. Season well. Sprinkle with vinegar. Place in a jar and refrigerate overnight. When ready to cook, place grillades (pork pieces) in skillet with melted margarine and brown on each side. Add onion, water to cover, and let simmer for 1 hour. Serve with grits and biscuits. (Serves 4)

CREOLE SALT PORK

(Te Sale)

Cut pieces of pork 2 inches thick, 6 inches long and 4 inches wide. In a crock, place a layer of coarse salt and then a layer of meat. Cover the meat with another layer of salt. Continue this process until all meat is used and all meat is covered with salt. Cover crock with muslin or similar.

Place in cool spot (not in refrigerator) until salt is melted and all meat is covered with brine (takes from 2 to 3 weeks.) Remove from crock, wash in warm water, dry and store in refrigerator or hang in kitchen.

Delicious with boiled cabbage, mustard greens, beans or good, as is, with pepper vinegar.

BARBECUED PORK RIBS with a SPECIAL CHINESE SAUCE

(Beer and honey glaze for ribs)

1 pork rib rack, about 6 pounds
1 cup Heinz chili sauce
½ cup Soy Sauce
Juice of ½ lemon
¼ teaspoon ginger, powdered
⅓ cup beer
⅓ cup honey

Combine ingredients and simmer for 20 minutes. Spread over barbecued spareribs during the last 30 minutes of cooking.

PORK BACKBONE STEW

4 pounds pork backbone pieces
1 stick margarine
4 tablespoons flour
1 large chopped onion
½ green bell pepper
2 stalks celery, chopped
2 cloves garlic, minced
1 tablespoon Worcestershire sauce
Tony's Creole Seasoning or salt and pepper
1 quart water
6 medium-size turnips (optional)

Make a roux with flour and margarine. Add chopped vegetables and saute for 1 or 2 minutes. Add pork backbone pieces, Tony's Creole Seasoning or salt and pepper, Worcestershire sauce and enough water to cover. Bring to boil, then let simmer until tender. If too thick, add more water. About 6 medium-sized turnips added with the backbone is good too.

Be sure to skim off excess fat. Serve with rice and the gravy. (Serves 8)

CHINESE PORK CHOPS

6 pork chops, 1 inch thick
1 teaspoon salt
¼ teaspoon black pepper
½ cup finely chopped onions
¼ cup finely chopped green bell peppers
2 8-ounce size cans tomato sauce
1 tablespoon Worcestershire sauce
⅓ cup wine vinegar
1 can (2½ cups) pineapple chunks and syrup
¼ cup brown sugar
½ teaspoon ground mustard

Season pork chops with salt and pepper. Place in shallow roasting pan and bake at 350 degrees for 45 minutes. Pour off all excess fat. While chops are roasting, mix remaining ingredients and let stand to blend flavor. Pour over chops and bake 45 minutes longer, basting frequently to glaze chops with the sauce. (Serves 6)

VEAL OSCAR

This recipe was graciously given to us by Executive Chef Hans John of the Shamrock Hilton, Houston, TX.

2-3 ounces veal
Salt, pepper
Flour
Sauce Bearnaise or Hollandaise
2 green asparagus spears
½ cup crawfish
¼ cup sliced mushrooms
¼ cup chopped onions
Oil

Season veal with salt and pepper, dust with flour and saute 2-3 minutes on both sides. Place veal on plate, cover with Sauce Bearnaise, place 2 asparagus spears on top of veal one inch apart and fill space with crawfish mixture.

CRAWFISH MIXTURE

Saute onions, mushrooms in butter until tender, add cooked crawfish, saute 5 more minutes, season and use -

SAUCE BEARNAISE

1 egg
¼ pound melted butter
Salt, white pepper
lemon juice
tarragon vinegar and chopped tarragon leaves

Mix egg, salt, pepper, lemon juice and tarragon vinegar in double boiler, whip until medium thickness, add butter in small amounts, beat constantly.

Do not boil water in double boiler or eggs will curdle. When butter is used up remove from boiler, add tarragon leaves and small amount brown sauce.

TONY'S BAKED PICNIC HAM

8 pound picnic ham (deboned)
8-ounce can crushed pineapple
1 small jar red cherries
½ pound brown sugar
1 tablespoon yellow mustard
1 tablespoon whole cloves

Have butcher debone ham and tie. Boil ham in water for one hour, remove and slice off skin. Score with diamond-shape cuts. Stud with whole cloves.

Place ham in open pan and bake for one hour. While ham is baking make a glaze with a mixture of pineapple juice, mustard and brown sugar. Cook slowly until thick.

After cooking ham one hour, spoon glaze over ham evenly then cover with crushed pineapple and decorate with cherries. Cook for 30 more minutes. Slice and serve. Uh-hum good! You never tasted anything so good.

JOHNSON'S BOUDIN BLANC

(White Boudin)

4 pounds fresh pork, ¼ fat
1 pound pork liver
Boiled rice (use 2 cups for each cup finished mixture)
3 cups basic vegetable mixture (see page 5)
1 cup chopped onion tops
½ cup fresh chopped parsley
1 package pork casings (from your local packing house)
Tony's Creole Seasoning

Run meat through meat grinder. Cover with water, bring to boil and simmer for 1 to 2 hours until well cooked. Pour off excess liquid and set aside. Mix meat with basic vegetable mix and onion tops and parsley; add to rice. Mix well and season on the hot side with Tony's Creole Seasoning. If too dry add liquid. Fill casings, tie ends. Place in boiling water for 30 minutes. Can also be used for a poultry dressing.

CREOLE HOGSHEAD CHEESE

1 hogs head (cut into 4 pieces, remove brains, ears, eyes and tissue)
4 hogs feet
3 pounds lean pork (fat removed)
½ sweet red pepper, or pimento, chopped
1 cup chopped onions
½ bell pepper, chopped
4 cloves garlic, minced
1 cup green onion tops and parsley, chopped
1 package plain gelatin
Tony's Creole Seasoning to taste (On the hot side)

Put head, feet, lean pork, garlic, bell pepper and onions in a large pot. Cover with water and boil until meat falls from bones. Remove meat and chop or grind. Cook remaining broth down to about 2 quarts or less. Strain, place meat and broth in saucepan. Season generously with Tony's Creole Seasoning. Add gelatin softened in a little water. Cook about 15 minutes. Add onion tops, red sweet pepper and parsley. Pour into soup bowls to mold. Place in refrigerator until it sets.

CREOLE SMOKED PORK SAUSAGE

3 pounds ground lean pork
1 pound pork fat
¼ teaspoon sugar
1 tablespoon powdered sage (optional)
Tony's Creole Seasoning

Mix thoroughly and stuff into casings or make into patties. Place in smoker over slow-burning green hickory and smoke until cured.

ISABELL'S COUNTRY STYLE CREOLE ROAST PORK

- 5 pound roast
- 1 cup basic vegetable mix (see page 5)
- ⅓ cup bacon fat
- 2 tablespoons Tony's Creole Seasoning (see page 3)

Punch about 10 slits in roast. Add 1 tablespoon Tony's seasoning to vegetable mixture, stuff slits equally. Use the other tablespoon Creole seasoning all over the roast, rub in well.

Place roast in Dutch oven (uncovered). Add bacon fat and cook in preheated oven at 350 degrees until roast is brown. Cover and cook at 300 degrees about three more hours, or until roast is tender. You can thicken gravy with a mixture of water and flour, if you want your gravy thicker. Skim off some of the excess fat. Be careful you don't eat too much, especially if you serve with boiled rice and gravy.

GRILLED SPARERIBS

- 3 to 4 pounds meaty spareribs
- Tony's Creole Seasoning or salt and pepper
- ¾ cup currant jelly
- 2 tablespoons port wine
- 1 tablespoon lemon juice
- 1 tablespoon dry mustard
- ½ teaspoon powdered ginger

Season ribs and place, meaty side up, on rack in shallow roasting pan. Roast in 450 degree oven 30 minutes. Melt jelly, add wine, lemon juice, mustard and ginger. Reduce oven to 350 degrees. Brush ribs with sauce every 15 minutes and continue baking 45 minutes to 1 hour or until tender.

OUTDOORS

Season ribs and place meaty side up on grill over slow coals. Broil about 20 minutes. Turn meaty side down and broil briefly until nicely brown. Turn meaty side up again and broil about 20 minutes longer. Brush meaty side with sauce and continue to broil without turning 20 to 30 minutes or until done, basting occasionally. (Serves 4)

SAVORY LAMB CHOPS

4 large lamb chops
14-ounce bottle catsup
Juice of 2 lemons
4 cloves garlic, minced
1 tablespoon Worcestershire
Tony's Creole Seasoning or salt and pepper to taste

Season lamb chops and place in a greased baking pan. Make a sauce with remaining ingredients and pour over chops. Place in 275-degree oven and bake 1½ hours. (Serves 4)

LAMB STEW with OLIVES

⅔ cup canned pitted ripe olives
3 pounds boneless lamb shoulder
2 tablespoons olive oil
1½ cups chopped onions
1 cup liquid from olives
1 teaspoon salt
¼ teaspoon black pepper
1 pound green string beans or 1 can
3 eggs
2 tablespoons cornstarch
¼ cup lemon juice

Drain ripe olives, reserving liquid. Cut lamb into small pieces. In heavy skillet heat oil and brown lamb pieces. Remove lamb from pot; add onions and cook until tender, but not brown. Add lamb, olive liquid, salt, pepper and bring to a boil. Reduce heat, cover and cook slowly about 1½ hours or until meat is almost tender.

Meanwhile, remove string from beans and cut into 2 inch pieces. Add olives and beans to meat and cook 12 to 20 minutes longer or until beans are tender. Beat eggs with cornstarch until light and beat in lemon juice. Slowly stir 1 cup of liquid from the stew into the egg blend; add to stew and cook over very low heat until mixture thickens, about 5 minutes. (Serves 6 to 8)

Serve with cooked Irish potatoes.

LAMB CHOPS in WINE SAUCE

4 large lamb chops
2 tablespoons cooking oil
1 cup honey
1 cup dry white wine
2 tablespoons Worcestershire
Tony's Creole Seasoning or salt and pepper
1 clove garlic, minced
½ teaspoon powdered ginger
4 drops Tabasco sauce

Season chops. Place oil in deep 12-inch skillet and brown chops slowly. Combine remaining ingredients, mix well and pour over chops. Simmer over low heat about 45 minutes. (Serves 4)

NOTE: Serve chops and sauce over hot-buttered noodles to which croutons and poppy seed have been added.

LAMB FRIES

(Mountain Oysters)

12 lamb fries
1 egg
1 cup milk
1 cup corn meal
Tony's Creole Seasoning or salt and pepper

Split lamb fries in half. Soak for 1 hour in mixture of milk and beaten egg. Season with Tony's Creole Seasoning, or salt and pepper, and dip in corn meal. Fry in deep fat at 375 degrees until brown. (Serves 4)

CREOLE SMOTHERED LIVER

1 pound calf liver
Tony's Creole Seasoning or salt and pepper
½ cup flour
1 cup hot water
2 tablespoons bacon drippings or oil
1 tablespoon minced green onions (scallions)

Cut liver in thin slices. Dip in boiling water for an instant, drain and make a few gashes in each side. Sprinkle with Tony's Creole Seasoning, or salt and pepper, and roll in flour. Shake off excess flour and fry in drippings for 5 minutes, turning once. Add 1 cup hot water and green onions. Reduce heat, cover skillet and smother until tender (about 15 minutes). Do not overcook. Serve with grits. (Serves 4)

BAKED LIVER and ONIONS

(With Bacon)

6 slices beef liver
6 slices bacon
2 large onions
¼ stick butter or margarine
½ cup dry red wine
¼ cup chopped parsley
1 bay leaf, crumbled
1 teaspoon thyme
½ cup flour
½ cup water
1 teaspoon salt
Freshly ground black pepper

Place 3 slices bacon on bottom of baking dish. Cut onions into ½-inch slices and arrange in baking dish on top of bacon. Add 3 slices bacon on top of onions and dot with butter. Add wine, parsley, bay leaf, thyme, salt, pepper and ½ cup water. Cover and bake in preheated oven (350 degrees) for 30 minutes.

Coat liver with flour, place on top of bacon and onion slices, cover and bake 30 minutes. Baste 2 or 3 times. Remove cover and bake 10 minutes. (Serves 6)   Try it!

ITALIAN ROLLETTES

Something wonderfully different to serve your family.

6 cube steaks, about 5 or 6 ounces each
1 teaspoon salt
¼ teaspoon pepper
3 tablespoons Wesson oil or olive oil
¼ cup chopped onions
2 eggs, well beaten
¼ cup chopped parsley
¼ cup grated Parmesan cheese
1 cup fresh bread crumbs

FOR SAUCE:

2 cans Hunt's, 6-ounce size tomato paste
1 cup hot water
1 clove garlic, minced
Tony's Creole Seasoning or salt and pepper
Pinch of basil or fresh basil leaf
8-ounce package spaghetti, cooked

Sprinkle steaks with salt and pepper. In Dutch oven, brown steaks in Wesson oil. Remove from heat and cool. Meanwhile, combine crumbs, onions, eggs, parsley and cheese. Mix lightly; spread evenly over steaks. Roll up and secure with toothpicks. Combine remaining ingredients, except spaghetti, and pour over steaks. Bring to boil, reduce heat, cover tightly and simmer 45 minutes or until tender. Remove toothpicks and serve with spaghetti. (Serves 6)

ITALIAN PIZZA

(Easy Way)

1 package Hot Roll Mix or 4 cups Biscuit Mix, made as for rolled biscuits
6-ounce can Hunt's tomato paste
½ cup hot water
1 teaspoon salt
Dash of pepper
½ teaspoon oregano or basil

Divide dough into 4 parts and roll in 9 inch circles. Place in oiled pie pans or cookie sheets. Dent here and there with fingertips and turn up edge. Brush with Wesson oil or olive oil. Mix Hunt's tomato paste with water and seasoning; spread over dough. Add your choice of toppings and dot with cheese. Bake in hot oven (450 degrees) 15 minutes or until dough is brown and crisp.

TOPPING: anchovies, mushrooms, pepperoni, salami, uncooked ground beef, chopped dried beef, sliced onions, chopped parsley, 1 lb. mozzarella or Swiss cheese, sliced thin. (Serves 4)

CHILI CON CARNE

½ pound beef suet
3 pounds coarsely ground chuck
2 large onions, chopped
4 cloves garlic, minced
6-ounce can tomato paste
4 tablespoons chili powder
1 teaspoon cumin
1 teaspoon oregano
Tony's Creole Seasoning or salt and pepper
4 cups beef stock (fresh or canned)
1½ cups freshly-cooked red kidney beans

Heat suet in deep fry pan or Dutch oven; add ground beef seasoned with Tony's Creole Seasoning or salt and pepper, onions and garlic. Fry meat until brown; add tomato paste, beef stock, cumin, chili powder, oregano and simmer slowly about 2 hours.

If you plan to use the beans, add to the Dutch oven 15 minutes before serving. (Serves 8)

TONY'S HE-MAN CHILI

1 pound hot sausage (Louisiana or Italian)
1 pound lean ground beef (chuck)
6 slices bacon
1 large onion (chopped)
1 bell pepper (cut up)
2 cloves garlic (minced)
Tony's Creole Seasoning to taste
1 Louisiana hot green pepper (or Jalapeno) diced
¼ cup Worcestershire sauce
1 cup Burgundy wine
1 teaspoon dry mustard
1 teaspoon celery seed
2 tablespoons chili powder
3 cups Italian pear tomatoes
1 (15-ounce) can pinto beans
2 (15-ounce) cans kidney beans

Brown bacon in large Dutch oven. Remove bacon, crumble and set aside. Slice sausage into one-inch pieces and fry in bacon fat until brown. Remove and set aside with bacon. Pour off excess fat and fry ground beef. Drain and set aside with other meat. Pour excess fat from pot. Cook onion, bell pepper, garlic and hot pepper over low heat 2 or 3 minutes. Stir in mustard, celery seeds, chili powder, simmer 10 minutes. Mash tomatoes, add with liquid and meats to onion mixture. Heat to boiling. Reduce heat and simmer, season to taste with Tony's Creole Seasoning; simmer for ½ hour, stirring occasionally.

Add beans with liquid, heat to boiling. Reduce heat and simmer for 1 hour, stirring occasionally. (Serves 10)

HOT TAMALE PIE

2 pounds ground beef
2 tablespoons cooking oil
6-ounce can tomato paste
2 onions, chopped
1 clove garlic, minced
1 large green bell pepper, chopped
1 cup celery, chopped
3 tablespoons chili powder
2 teaspoons red pepper
1 teaspoon salt
1 cup corn meal
3 cups water

Fry ground beef in oil in a deep 12-inch skillet. Add chopped vegetables, saute 5 minutes, then add tomato paste, seasoning to taste and cook 5 more minutes. Add 1 cup of water and simmer for 1 hour.

In another container mix corn meal with cold water. Skim oil from top of meat, add to corn meal mixture and salt to taste. Cook 20 minutes then combine with meat mixture and add balance of salt and red pepper.

Place in casserole baking dish and cook over a hot water bath for 2 hours. (Serves 8)

TONY'S MEAT BALLS and SPAGHETTI

(I've tried them all and this is it)

1 pound ground lean meat (½ pork, ½ beef)
1 cup olive oil
½ cup cracker meal (or 10 crackers)
3 eggs (well beaten)
1 tablespoon chopped parsley
½ cup chopped green onion tops (scallions)
¼ cup grated Romano cheese
Tony's Creole Seasoning or salt and pepper
1 cup milk

To make meat balls add to meat: cracker meal, eggs, parsley, onion tops, cheese, seasoning, and enough milk to make a soft mixture. Wet hands with water and roll into 10 very soft meat balls (add water to mixture if not soft enough). Fry in olive oil in heavy Dutch oven until brown. Remove from pot and set aside.

SAUCE

2 cans tomato paste
1 large chopped onion
2 cloves garlic
½ bell pepper
1 tablespoon sugar
1 fresh basil leaf, or equal
10 or more anise seeds to taste (faint)
Tony's Creole Seasoning or salt and pepper

Add to the olive oil, in Dutch oven, the chopped onion, garlic, bell pepper and saute until brown. Add the tomato paste and cook for another 10 minutes. Add the sugar, basil and anise with enough water to cook down to right consistency (about 1 quart). Cook 3 hours, then add meat balls and cook slowly for another 2 hours (use judgment). Bring seasoning up to taste, skim off excess fat, pour over spaghetti and serve. (Serves 6)

NOTE: To make tender meat balls be sure you add enough milk or water so that meat balls barely hold their shape.

Spaghetti boiled in hot, salted chicken broth does wonders for your spaghetti dish.

SWEETBREADS en BROCHETTE

3 pairs of sweetbreads
1 egg beaten
1 tablespoon of dry white wine
½ cup of bread crumbs
6 slices of bacon cut in pieces
24 mushroom caps
3 medium green peppers, cut in 1-inch squares
½ cup of butter, melted
½ teaspoon salt
Freshly ground black pepper

Cut each parboiled sweetbread into 4 pieces. Dip in egg beaten with wine, salt and pepper. Then dip in bread crumbs. Place on skewers, alternating sweetbreads with bacon, mushrooms and peppers. Broil on a low heat, basting with melted butter until golden brown. (Serves 6)

TRIPE CREOLE

2 pounds fresh tripe, cleaned
4 tablespoons butter or margarine
2 onions, thinly sliced
1 large clove garlic, minced
¼ cup finely chopped lean ham
6 tomatoes, peeled and coarsely chopped
1 green bell pepper, thinly diced
Tony's Creole Seasoning or salt and pepper

Wash tripe thoroughly in cold water, drain. Put in a saucepan and add salted water to cover. (1 teaspoon salt per quart of water.) Bring to boiling, reduce heat and simmer covered, about 5 hours or until tender. Drain tripe, cut into 2x2-inch strips and set aside.

Heat butter in a heavy saucepan, add onions, garlic and cook until golden. Add remaining ingredients and season to taste. Bring to boiling and cook for 10 minutes, stirring occasionally.

Add tripe, bring to boiling, cover and cook 30 minutes. (Serves 6 to 8)

CREAMED SWEETBREADS with MUSHROOMS

2 pairs sweetbreads
4-ounce can sliced mushrooms
2 tablespoons margarine
Tony's Creole Seasoning or salt and pepper
2 tablespoons flour
1 pint pure cream
2 tablespoons dry white wine

Clean and parboil sweetbreads for 20 minutes. Remove all pipes and membranes and chop into 2-inch pieces. Melt margarine in saucepan, add flour and when smooth, add cream and stir until mixture boils. Add mushrooms, let simmer about 5 minutes. Add sweetbreads, wine, seasoning and cook for 5 minutes longer. Serve on buttered toast. (Serves 4)

CREOLE STYLE SWEETBREADS

1 pair sweetbreads, about 1 pound
1 tablespoon lemon juice
2 tablespoons flour
¼ teaspoon salt
½ teaspoon paprika
3 tablespoons fat
1 cup thin cream
Chopped parsley

Soak sweetbreads in cold water for 2 hours. Drain. Cover with boiling water, add lemon juice and cook, covered, for 20 minutes or until tender. Do not overcook. Drain and immediately plunge into ice water and let stand 10 minutes.

Remove all pipes and membranes. Cut each sweetbread in half crosswise. Mix flour and seasonings. Coat sweetbread with the mix. Pan fry in hot fat, cooking slowly until delicately browned and glazed. Remove to heated platter.

Scrape loose brown bits from skillet, add cream, cook and stir over low heat until slightly thickened. Add few drops lemon juice and a little parsley. Pour over sweetbreads and serve on toast. (Serves 4)

PONCE BOURRÉ

1 pork stomach
(table ready)
1 stick margarine

Use white boudin mixture, page 101 and stuff stomach (ponce). Melt margarine in Dutch oven or baking pan. Baste ponce with melted margarine. Bake in 300-degree oven for 1 hour or until outside is brown and crisp. Make gravy with pan drippings.

OPELOUSAS BAKED LONG ISLAND DUCK

(Not Duckling)

1 duck, 5 to 7 pounds,
cut in half
1 cup oil
1 cup water
1 small can paprika
Tony's Creole Seasoning
or salt and pepper

Season duck halves generously with Tony's Creole Seasoning or salt and pepper. Sprinkle, skin side up, with paprika and place in an open baking pan.

Over the halves, pour mixture of oil and water. Cook in a preheated oven (275 degrees) 3 to 5 hours, basting every half hour. Remove duck halves, pour off excess fat and save for next cooking.

NOTE: If you save this left-over fat and use the next time you cook duck, it will be much better.

Long, slow cooking, along with the basting, is the secret. Of course, the seasoning has everything to do with the taste. Pan drippings can be used in rice dressing also.

OPELOUSAS BAKED CHICKEN

4 fryer halves
Tony's Creole Seasoning or salt and pepper
1 cup leftover chicken fat or oil
1 cup water
1 can paprika (small)
1 teaspoon chili powder

Season chicken generously with Tony's Creole Seasoning or salt and pepper. Rub well on each side. Place fryer halves in open baking pan and cover with a mixture of oil and water. Place pan in pre-heated oven (275 degrees) and cook until hot. Sprinkle generously with paprika and chili powder. Baste continuously about every half hour until dark, dark brown. Takes 3 to 5 hours.

NOTE: This is a very famous Opelousas dish. The secret is in the seasoning and the long, slow basting process. It's served with rice dressing, petit pois, candied yams, and green salad, French bread and black coffee demi-tasse. (Serves 4)

TONY'S OLD FASHIONED CHICKEN STEW

1 fat hen or rooster (about 6 pounds) cut up to fry
¾ cup milk
½ cup flour
1 stick margarine
1 onion, chopped fine
2 sticks celery, chopped
1 green bell pepper, chopped
3 cloves garlic, chopped fine
1 tablespoon Worcestershire
Tony's Creole Seasoning or salt and pepper

Season chicken with Tony's Creole Seasoning. Melt margarine in Dutch oven. Dip chicken in milk, then flour, and fry in margarine until brown. Remove chicken.

Saute onion, celery, bell pepper and garlic in pot until tender. Add chicken and enough water to cover. Add Worcestershire sauce, cover, and cook slowly until tender. Takes about 4 hours. Serve with boiled rice or spaghetti. (Serves 8)

TONY'S BREADED FRIED CHICKEN

3-pound fryer cut in 8 pieces and skinned
¼ cup fresh lemon juice
1½ cups bread crumbs
½ cup flour
½ pound shortening
1 egg lightly beaten
Lemon wedges
Tony's Creole Seasoning or salt and pepper

In a glass bowl toss chicken with the lemon juice. Marinate about 1½ hours, turning the pieces occasionally. Before frying, pat dry with paper towels. Season generously.

Dip chicken in flour and shake off excess, then dip in egg. Roll each piece of chicken in bread crumbs to coat thoroughly.

In a heavy 12-inch skillet, heat shortening to about 375 degrees. Using tongs, add one-half the chicken pieces. When golden brown on one side, turn them with tongs. When browned, transfer to paper towels to drain before serving. Serve chicken garnished with lemon wedges. (Serves 4)

TONY'S CRISPY FRIED CHICKEN

2½ to 3-pound fryer
1 tablespoon Tony's Famous Creole Seasoning
1 cup rich milk
2 eggs
2 cups all-purpose flour
1 quart cooking oil or shortening in your favorite deep fat fryer

Cut chicken in usual size pieces. Season all over generously with Tony's seasoning (see page 3). Make a batter with one can evaporated milk or one cup rich milk and two eggs. Marinate chicken pieces for at least 10 minutes. Remove, dip in flour and fry in preheated deep fat fryer at 380 degrees for at least 30 minutes, until golden brown and crispy tender.

TONY'S CHICKEN SAUTE AUX GROS ONIONS and OLIVES

(Chicken Smothered in Onions)

2 large fryers, cut up
2 large onions, thinly sliced
1 medium green pepper, chopped
1 can mushrooms
½ can black ripe olives
1 cup cooking oil
⅓ cup flour
Tony's Creole Seasoning to taste

Season chicken well with Tony's Famous Creole seasoning, place in hot cooking oil and brown. Sprinkle flour on pieces while browning. When all are browned, place back in Dutch oven and add sliced onions, olives, mushrooms and chopped green peppers. Cover and cook under low fire until chicken is tender. When ready to serve, add a little water to gravy. Serve with boiled rice and French bread.

BROILED CHICKEN LIVERS with BACON and WATER CHESTNUTS

12 chicken livers
1 small can water chestnuts
6 slices bacon

Wrap each water chestnut with a chicken liver, then with ½ slice of bacon and secure with a toothpick. Fry in deep fat until bacon is crisp, or use a skewer and fry over hot coals. Serve with Chinese Brown Sauce and Chinese Hot Mustard Sauce. (See pages 14 and 15)

PAELLA

(Chicken and Rice with Almonds, Olives and Mushrooms)

2 tablespoons olive oil
3-pound chicken
2 teaspoons salt
½ teaspoon black pepper
6 small onions, peeled
2 cloves garlic, minced
2½ cups raw rice
1 cup dry white wine
5 cups chicken stock
1 teaspoon oregano
½ stick margarine
3½ ounces blanched almonds
¾ cup chopped olives
4-ounce can mushrooms, quartered
⅛ teaspoon saffron, enough to color rice bright yellow

Preheat oven to 325 degrees. Heat olive oil in a Dutch oven; add chicken, cut into serving portions, and sprinkle with salt and pepper. Cook in a moderate oven, uncovered, for 15 minutes; add onions and cook for 45 minutes. Add garlic and raw rice, mix well. Add 1 cup wine and 3 cups chicken stock. Cover and cook for 45 minutes longer, then color with saffron.

Season with salt and pepper, sprinkle with oregano, almonds and olives. Add 2 cups of chicken stock to mixture and keep hot in oven.

Saute mushrooms in margarine for 5 minutes. Sprinkle on top of Paella and serve hot with a tossed green salad. (Serves 6)

JAPANESE CHICKEN-PORK BARBECUE

1 half-baked chicken
2 pounds pork chops, half-cooked
Onion
Green bell pepper
½ cup soy sauce
2 tablespoons honey
1 tablespoon sherry wine
1 clove crushed garlic

Cut up chicken and pork chops in 1-inch pieces. Place on skewer in this order: 1 piece chicken, 1 piece onion, 1 piece pork, 1 piece bell pepper. Continue until 8 pieces of meat are on skewer.

Dip in mixture of soy sauce, honey, sherry and garlic. Broil over hot coals.

Very, very good. I picked this one up at the World's Fair in New York.

DEE'S CHICKEN and SPAGHETTI

5 to 6-pound hen
1 No. 2 can whole tomatoes
1 No. 2 can mushrooms
4-ounce bottle olive oil
Tony's Creole Seasoning or salt and pepper
1 teaspoon poultry seasoning
2 large onions, chopped
2 large green bell peppers, chopped
5 ribs celery, chopped
2 cloves garlic, minced
2 cans tomato paste, 6-ounce size
1 cup Romano cheese, grated
1 No. 4 package spaghetti
Salt

Boil or pressure cook hen until thoroughly cooked. Debone and reserve stock. Saute onions, bell pepper, garlic and celery in olive oil. Add tomatoes, tomato paste and 1 quart chicken stock. Add Tony's Creole Seasoning (or salt and pepper) and poultry seasoning. Allow to cook slowly for 3 hours adding stock if necessary. Add ½ cup cheese during last half-hour of cooking, together with mushrooms and cooked chicken.

Boil spaghetti in salted water for 12 minutes. Place in collander, rinse in cold water, drain well. Add sauce to cooked spaghetti and allow to stand until time to serve. Offer additional cheese when serving. (Serves 8)

PIGEONNEAUX en PARADIS

6 squab
1 stick margarine, melted
1 cup chopped celery
½ cup chopped onions
½ cup chopped carrots
Tony's Creole Seasoning or salt and pepper
2 cups Wild Game Sauce (See page 13)

Season squab well inside and out. Rub with margarine. Combine vegetables: add 1 tablespoon to inside of each squab, balance on bottom of deep baking pan or in casserole. Place squab in pan and pour Game Sauce over squab, cover and bake in 350-degree oven for 30 minutes or until tender. (Serves 6)

TONY'S ROAST TURKEY

Everybody knows how to roast a turkey. There are 50 different ways to do it, and they are all good. But very few people know how to season a turkey to bring out that real turkey flavor — juicy, tender and flavorful. The secret is in the seasoning and the seasoning is Tony's Famous Creole Seasoning.

12 to 14-pound turkey
2 to 3 tablespoons Tony's seasoning
2 strips bacon
½ (10-ounce) jar currant jelly
1 cup Basic Vegetable Mix (see page 5)
8-ounce can mushroom stems and pieces
2 sticks margarine or butter
1 cup chicken stock or broth
1 cup onion tops and parsley (chopped)

Season turkey inside and out generously with Tony's seasoning. Place 1 cup vegetable mix and 1 stick margarine inside turkey. Place turkey in baking pan, cover turkey breast with bacon strips, pour the chicken broth, half inside turkey and the other half in bottom of baking pan. Cover. Place in 300-degree preheated oven and bake 3 to 4 hours, steaming until tender. Remove cover, pour off pan juices, set oven to 500 degrees and brown. Watch closely, it takes only 10 minutes.

To the pan juices add 1 cup onion tops and parsley chopped fine. Use the juice of an 8-ounce can of mushroom stems and pieces and add 2 tablespoons flour. Mix and add to pan juices. Cook for 5 minutes until juice thickens into a beautiful brown gravy. Add Kitchen Bouquet if not brown enough. Add ½ jar currant jelly if you like your gravy a little sweet.

Ideal size for family of eight. If there's any left over, you can finish it off with turkey sandwiches. If you like this, tell me about it.

CASSEROLE of GUINEA HEN with BRANDY SAUCE

3 pound guinea hen
1 stick butter
¼ cup Basic Vegetable Mixture (see page 5)
½ cup cooking oil
1½ cups chicken stock
¼ cup Burgundy wine
1 chicken bouillon cube
Tony's Creole Seasoning to taste
1 clove garlic
1 tablespoon currant jelly
1 tablespoon pure cream or sour cream
1 tablespoon cornstarch
½ cup water
1 ounce brandy

Preheat oven to moderate 375 degrees. Take one oven-ready guinea hen, rub lightly inside and out with Tony's Creole Seasoning. Inside the cavity place ½ stick butter and ¼ cup basic vegetable mixture, then brush with melted butter and cooking oil. Put bird on its back in shallow roasting pan and place in moderately hot oven. After 10 minutes baste with melted butter and cooking oil, and turn on its side. Repeat basting and turning every 10 minutes. In 30 minutes bird should be golden brown. Reduce oven heat to 300 degrees.

Transfer guinea hen to small oval casserole with tight fitting cover. Add one tablespoon butter and ½ cup chicken stock. Cover and place in 300-degree oven for 20 minutes.

Pour off all cooking fat from roasting pan, being careful not to lose the brown drippings. Place over medium heat and add Burgundy. Stir to lift drippings; add three-fourths cup chicken stock, chicken bouillon cube, 1 tablespoon butter, garlic, currant jelly and cream. Stir well to blend and bring to a boil. If sauce needs fixing dissolve one tablespoon cornstarch and ½ cup water and add to sauce, little by little, stirring constantly. Stop when sauce is thick enough. Strain sauce over guinea hen in casserole. Sprinkle brandy over all and serve piping hot. You can do the same with duck, chicken or goose. (Serves 6)

TONY'S BAKED CORNISH GAME HENS

6 Cornish game hens (14 to 20 ounces)
1 stick margarine or butter
1 cup chicken broth
½ cup Basic Vegetable Mixture (see page 5)
3 strips bacon
8-ounce can mushroom stems and pieces
1 tablespoon Worcestershire sauce
½ cup chopped green onion tops and parsley
1 heaping tablespoon flour
2 heaping tablespoons currant jelly
3 tablespoons Tony's Seasoning (see page 3)

Season inside and out the Cornish hens generously with Tony's Seasoning. Stuff inside birds with equal parts margarine and vegetable mix. Place in baking dish breast side up. Layer with bacon slices. Pour 1 cup chicken broth in pan with birds. Cover pan with aluminum foil and bake in preheated 325-degree oven for at least 1½ hours until birds are tender. Remove foil, pour off pan juices into skillet on top of stove. Replace birds in oven. Raise to 500 degrees and watch closely until brown. To the pan juices in skillet, add onion tops and parsley. Make a mixture with the juice from the mushrooms, and flour. Add mushrooms and mixture to skillet juices, also add the currant jelly at this time. Cook and stir for about 5 minutes until gravy thickens. Pour gravy over each bird and serve one bird to each person. Serve with petit pois, corn bread dressing, broccoli casserole, green salad and French bread.

A lady called me up the other day. She sounded real mad. She said I had to take this recipe out of my book. I told her I thought it was a very good recipe. "That's the trouble." she said. "I cooked this for my son the other day and he ate so much I thought he was going to die!"

CORNISH HENS with BASTING SAUCE

4 Cornish hens, cleaned and dressed, placed on rotisserie over hot coals. (Serves 6 to 8)

Make sauce with the following:

¾ cup finely chopped onions
1 clove garlic, minced
¼ cup salad oil or olive oil
12-ounce can pear nectar
½ cup white wine vinegar
¼ cup honey
2 tablespoons Worcestershire
1 teaspoon prepared horseradish
1 teaspoon dry mustard
1 teaspoon salt
½ teaspoon thyme
¼ teaspoon rosemary
¼ teaspoon black pepper

In a saucepan cook onion and garlic in hot oil until tender. Do not brown. Add remaining ingredients; simmer uncovered for 5 minutes. Use as marinade or for basting while cooking on rotisserie. Serve remaining sauce on table. (Makes 3½ cups)

CHACHERE'S DEEP FRIED TURKEY

14 Lb. Turkey (approx.)

Mix the following ingredients in blender two days before cooking and refrigerate.

1 tablespoon Worcestershire sauce
2 tablespoons mustard
3-2 ounce bottles garlic juice
3-2 ounce bottles onion juice
3 ounces hot sauce
2 ounces Tony Cachere's Creole Seasoning
8 ounces of water or inch from top of blender

Directions:

Inject turkey inside and out with a syringe using all mixture from the blender. When completed, rub turkey with mustard and season generously with creole seasoning.

When ready to cook, heat approximately 5 gallons peanut oil to 300°, submerge turkey and let fry for 5 minutes, then immediately turn heat to low and cook for an additional 55 minutes.

TONY CHACHERE'S

LOUISIANA'S ORIGINAL CREOLE

SEAFOOD RECIPES

$9.95

A Complete Coverage of All Louisiana's Bountiful Seafood Recipes

Plus Gourmet Cooking at its Best

VEGETABLES AND CASSEROLES

TONY CHACHERE'S CREOLE SEAFOOD SAUCE

For oysters, shrimp, crab meat, crawfish, lobster and all seafood.

For a real Creole Sauce chop 1 cup celery fine, mix with one cup Tony Chachere's Creole Seafood Sauce. Pour over or mix with seafood. To serve with oysters on half shell, place one fresh opened oyster on a cracker. Cover with sauce and eat. Makes a great dip.

LOUISIANA YAM, COCONUT and ORANGE CASSEROLE

4 medium-sized Louisiana yams, cooked and peeled or 2 cans (16 ounces each) Louisiana yams, drained
2 eggs
¼ cup margarine, melted
½ cup brown sugar
¾ teaspoon salt
¼ teaspoon cinnamon
2 tablespoons rum
⅔ cup shredded coconut
1 tablespoon margarine, melted
Orange sections for garnish

Mash yams in large mixing bowl. Add eggs, ¼ cup butter, sugar, salt, cinnamon and rum. Beat until mixture is light and fluffy. Turn into greased shallow casserole or 1-quart baking dish. Bake at 325 degrees for 35 minutes.

Toss coconut with 1 tablespoon melted margarine. Sprinkle a border of coconut around edge of casserole. Arrange orange sections inside border. Bake 10 to 15 minutes more until coconut browns slightly. (Serves 6)

SPICED, BAKED LOUISIANA YAMS

4 medium-sized Louisiana yams, cooked, peeled or halved or 1 can (1 pound) Louisiana yams, drained and halved
⅓ cup melted margarine
¼ teaspoon ginger
½ teaspoon nutmeg
¼ cup brown sugar

Arrange yams in shallow baking dish. Combine margarine, ginger, nutmeg and sugar. Mix well and pour mixture over yams, bake in moderate oven (350 degrees) for 30 minutes. (Serves 4)

FRENCH-FRIED SWEET POTATOES

Peel raw sweet potatoes and cut into ½ to ¾-inch strips. Soak in cold, salted water for a short time; drain and dry between towels. Fry in deep fat (365 degrees) 3 to 5 minutes until brown. Drain on absorbent paper and sprinkle lightly with salt. Serve with pork chops, steaks, ham, etc.

Opelousas is the home of the Louisiana Yambilee, the national sweet potato festival held every October at harvest time. The two recipes following were judged best over-all dishes in the 1971 Yambilee.

First Prize Adult Winner: Mrs. Brice Palmer

YUMMY LOUISIANA PRODUCE BAKE

2 cups diced cooked ham
2 cups diced cooked chicken
¼ cup butter or margarine
¼ cup enriched flour
3-ounce can broiled, sliced drained mushrooms
1 cup chicken broth from cooked chicken
1 cup light cream
¼ cup grated onion
Dash cayenne pepper
8 yam dumplings

Place diced ham and chicken in a 2-quart casserole. Melt butter in a pot; blend in flour. Stir in cream and broth. Cook and stir until thick. Add seasonings, onions, mushrooms. Pour over ham and chicken.

Top ham mixture with dumplings. Bake in moderate 350-degree oven about 45 minutes. When cooked, garnish with parsley sprigs in center of casserole. (Make 6 to 8 servings)

YAM DUMPLINGS: Combine 1 cup mashed, cooked Louisiana yams, one-third cup melted butter and 1 beaten egg. Sift together 1 cup enriched flour, 2 teaspoons baking powder, ½ teaspoon salt, ½ teaspoon cinnamon. Blend into yams; drop by teaspoonful on top of hot casserole.

First Prize Junior Winner: Christine Champagne

YAM HOLIDAY PARTY CANDLE CAKES

5 cups Louisiana yams (grated raw)
4½ cups sugar
1 teaspoon vanilla
1 cup high grade salad oil
4 eggs, separated
½ teaspoon cinnamon
2½ teaspoons nutmeg
1 teaspoon salt
3½ cups sifted flour
2 teaspoons soda diluted with ⅔ cup water
2 cups chopped nuts
½ cup raisins
½ cup coconut
1 cup cane syrup
8 to 10 vegetable soup cans

Cook yams with 1½ cups sugar about 3 minutes. Cool. Add vanilla and set aside. Cream remaining sugar with oil. Add egg yolks and spice. Sift some of the flour into bowl and mix. Continue to add flour little by little until all has been blended. Mix soda with water and add to batter along with salt, nuts, raisins, syrup and coconut. Stir in yam mixture. Beat egg whites and fold into batter.

Use soup cans to form candles. Grease cans generously. Pour batter into cans leaving ¾-inch space for rising. Bake at 350 degrees for one hour. Makes about 60 party servings.

ORANGE CANDIED SWEET POTATOES

6 medium-sized sweet potatoes
1 cup orange juice
½ teaspoon grated orange rind
1 cup water
1 cup sugar
¼ cup butter
½ teaspoon salt

Peel and slice uncooked potatoes in ¼ inch slices and arrange in a buttered baking dish. Make a syrup of the ingredients and pour over potatoes. Cover and bake in moderate oven until tender. Baste occasionally. Remove lid the last 10 minutes, allow to brown. If desired, a layer of marshmallows may be added and browned just before removing from the oven. (Serves 6)

BAKED GOLDEN LOUISIANA YAMS

Select 1 dozen medium-size yams, wash and dry thoroughly. Do not remove jackets. Rub jackets with cooking oil and place in open baking pan. Bake in pre-heated 400-degree oven for 2 hours or until tender. Peel and serve with your favorite meal or eat as is. Cajuns like them with homemade vegetable soup or gumbo.

CABBAGE and FRESH PORK SAUSAGE

1 pound fresh pork sausage
1 pound boiled cabbage
1 egg, well beaten

Cook sausage in skillet half-filled with water until all water is cooked out and sausage is well done, but not brown. Add cabbage, drained and cut in small pieces. Let cook slowly and just before serving, add the egg. Cook 5 minutes longer and serve with cornbread. (Serves 8)

TONY'S CABBAGE CASSEROLE

1 medium head cabbage
1 pound ground lean meat
¼ cup green onions, chopped
1 medium onion, chopped
2 cloves garlic, minced
10½-ounce can cream of mushroom soup
1 cup boiled rice
¼ cup bread crumbs
Tony's Creole Seasoning to taste
½ stick margarine

Cut cabbage as you would to smother and boil in salted water until tender, but still green. Drain and reserve the liquid. Melt the margarine in a deep skillet and fry ground meat with onions, garlic and Tony's Creole Seasoning until brown. Mix cabbage with the meat, adding mushroom soup, green onion tops and boiled rice.

Pour into greased flat Pyrex baking dish. Top with bread crumbs and bake for 20 to 30 minutes at 300 degrees. Before baking, if you think it is too dry you can add some of the water from the boiled cabbage or another can of mushroom soup.

Very good!

STUFFED CABBAGE ROLLS

1 medium head firm cabbage
1 pound ground beef
¼ pound ground ham
1 cup cooked rice
1 egg, well beaten
1 onion, chopped fine
½ cup milk
Tony's Creole Seasoning or salt and pepper
½ cup water
1 cup Basic Tomato Sauce (See page 6)

Clean cabbage and remove core. Steam or boil cabbage until leaves are wilted and pliable. Separate leaves. Reserve 8 to 10 of the largest for rolls.

Thoroughly mix beef, ham, rice, egg, onion, milk and seasoning. Fill each leaf separately with mixture. Wrap leaf securely, envelope-fashion, and skewer with toothpicks.

Place flat down in Dutch oven or heavy saucepan. Add water, Basic Tomato Sauce and place remaining leaves on top. Cover tightly and cook over low heat for 1½ hours. Add small amount of water if necessary. (Serves 8-10)

ESCALLOPED CABBAGE

3 cups cooked cabbage
1 cup white sauce (medium thick)
½ cup grated cheese
Bread crumbs, buttered
Salt and pepper to taste

Shred cabbage and remove hard parts. Cook in boiling salted water until tender, about 7 to 10 minutes. Add grated cheese to white sauce just before removing from the fire and pour over cabbage in buttered dish. Cover with buttered bread crumbs and brown in oven.

FRIED EGGPLANT CASSEROLE

2 eggplants
2 cups grated bread
¼ cup grated Romano and Parmesan cheese
¼ cup chopped parsley
Salt and pepper
1 pod garlic
2 eggs, slightly beaten
Olive oil for frying
1 can stewed tomatoes

Peel eggplant and slice into ¼-inch round slices. Dip into eggs then into bread crumbs that have been mixed with cheese and seasoning. Fry in olive oil until golden brown. Drain. Layer in square 9-inch casserole with stewed tomatoes. Bake 15 to 20 minutes at 350 degrees or until heated through. May be prepared ahead of time, ready to slip into oven for company.

STUFFED EGGPLANT

Choose 3 small firm eggplants. Cut lengthwise and parboil 5 minutes in boiling salted water. Drain. Scoop out the pulp and mix with the following:

1 small onion, chopped
½ green bell pepper, chopped and cooked first in butter
½ cup cooked rice
½ cup chopped ham or tongue, bacon, chicken or mixture of all

Salt and pepper to taste. Fill shell with this mixture and bake in a moderate oven until shell is tender and top is brown. (Makes 6 servings.)

FRIED EGGPLANTS

2 eggplants
1 egg
1 cup milk
Tony's Creole Seasoning
or salt and pepper
Bread crumbs, flour or
cornmeal
Cooking oil

Peel eggplants and slice in rounds. Soak in salted water for ½ hour and drain. Beat egg and combine with milk. Dip eggplant in mixture, remove and roll in seasoned bread crumbs, flour or cornmeal. Fry in deep fat until golden brown and drain on absorbent paper. (Serves 4 to 6)

EGGPLANT with SHRIMP CASSEROLE

2 eggplants
2 medium onions,
chopped
½ cup celery, chopped
1 medium bell pepper,
chopped
¼ cup minced parsley
4 pods garlic, chopped
1 cup bread
Milk or water
2 teaspoons basil
1 teaspoon sage
Dash of Tabasco
1 teaspoon rosemary
2 eggs
1 teaspoon lemon juice
Tony's Creole Seasoning
Dash of red pepper
¼ cup grated Romano
cheese
2 strips bacon
2 pounds shrimp, cleaned
and deveined

Peel, cut and soak eggplant in salt water 30 minutes. Meanwhile fry bacon, remove, crumble and set aside. Saute shrimp in bacon drippings 3 minutes. Soak bread in milk or water, then squeze. Mix all ingredients, season to taste,and reserve half the cheese to sprinkle on top. Place in buttered casserole and add remaining cheese. Bake in 350-degree oven for 45 minutes.

EGGPLANT, CRABMEAT CASSEROLE

1 large eggplant
1 large onion, chopped
1 pound fresh cleaned shrimp
¼ stick margarine
1 cup bread crumbs
1 cup cooked crab meat
Tony's Creole Seasoning to taste

Peel, cut and dice eggplant and soak in seasoned water. Cook onion in margarine until wilted. Add raw shrimp and continue cooking over medium heat until onion browns slightly. Add eggplant and cook slowly until very tender. Add crab meat and most of the bread crumbs. Moisten these and mix well.

Cook over low heat to dressing consistency. Put in a casserole, sprinkle with bread crumbs and bake in 350-degree oven until lightly brown. (Serves 4)

SEAFOOD CASSEROLE

1½ pounds boiled shrimp, cleaned
1 pound crabmeat
1 bell pepper
1 onion
½ cup onion tops
½ cup parsley
3 cloves garlic
½ cup celery
2 cups cooked rice
2 cans mushroom soup
Tabasco to taste
3 tablespoons Worcestershire
Tony's Creole Seasoning

Chop all seasonings fine. Combine all ingredients, season to taste, and place in a greased casserole and bake at low temperature about 45 minutes. Decorate top of baked casserole with red or Jalapeno peppers. (More pepper can be added to other ingredients before baking if highly seasoned food is desired.)

TONY'S CRABMEAT CASSEROLE

2 lbs. crabmeat
6 green onions and tops, chopped
4 pods garlic, chopped
4 tablespoons parsley, chopped
1 stick oleo
Half & Half cream
Black pepper
2 tablespoons minced green pepper
1 teaspoon celery salt
8 slices toast
Bread crumbs
2 eggs
Tony's Creole Seasoning to taste

Saute chopped green onions and tops, garlic, parsley, green peppers in one stick oleo in a covered pan until soft. Add celery salt. Roll toast in bread crumbs and pull into small pieces and mix well with above. Add 2 well beaten eggs. Add crabmeat and enough Half & Half cream to moisten. Add Tony's Creole Seasoning to taste. Cover with buttered bread crumbs and bake in two buttered quart and a half casserole dishes for 30 minutes at 375 degrees, uncovered. (Serves 10)

You may substitute crawfish, lobster or shrimp. Can also be used as a hot dip.

FRIED OKRA

1 pound tender okra
½ cup milk
1 egg
1 cup cornmeal
Tony's Creole Seasoning or salt and pepper
Cooking oil

Cut tender, young okra in 1-inch rounds and season to taste. In a small bowl beat egg and add milk. Dip okra in mixture and roll in seasoned cornmeal. Fry in deep fat until crisp and brown. Drain on absorbent paper. Tastes like fried oysters. (Serves 4)

MAQUECHOU

12 ears tender, fresh corn
1 large onion, chopped
1 green bell pepper, chopped
1 fresh tomato, diced small
1 clove garlic, minced
1 cup milk
1 stick margarine
Tony's Creole Seasoning or salt and pepper

Cut corn off cob and scrape cobs to get all the juice. Heat margarine in Dutch oven, add onion, bell pepper, garlic and saute until tender. Add corn, tomato, season to taste, and cook mixture over medium heat for 1½ hours. Stir constantly adding a little milk from time to time to keep mixture soft. (Serves 6)

NOTE: to make CHICKEN MAQUECHOU

3-pound fryer, cut in pieces
Tony's Creole Seasoning or salt and pepper to taste
1 cup milk
1 egg, well beaten
1 cup flour
Oil or drippings for frying

Season chicken. Combine egg and milk; dip chicken in mixture; dredge in flour and shake off excess. Fry in oil or drippings until done and add to Maquechou. Mix well and serve.

FRIED GREEN TOMATOES

4 medium-sized green tomatoes
Salt and pepper to taste
1 cup cornmeal
2 tablespoons bacon drippings or equal

Cut tomatoes in quarters, add salt and pepper to taste, and let stand about ½ hour. Drain juice, dip tomatoes in cornmeal and fry in bacon drippings. Add more fat, if necessary, to keep from burning. Brown on both sides and place on absorbent paper. (Serves 4)

Squash and okra may be fried the same way.

TONY'S MEAT and SPAGHETTI CASSEROLE

1 pound ground beef
1 can tomatoes
1 can tomato paste
1 large onion
3 sticks celery
1 clove garlic
1 bay leaf
½ chopped green pepper
⅛ teaspoon oregano
⅛ teaspoon thyme
⅛ teaspoon salt
½ pound spaghetti, boiled in salted water
½ pound sharp cheese
Oil for browning

Brown onions, garlic, celery, pepper in DUTCH OVEN. To this add tomatoes and tomato paste, bay leaf, oregano and thyme. Stir in ground beef and cook slowly, about two hours. Add water as needed. Combine sauce and spaghetti and put into greased baking dish. Top with sharp cheese and heat in 375-degree oven until cheese melts.

TOMATO and BACON CASSEROLE

8 slices bacon
2 bell peppers
2 small onions
2 large cans tomatoes
1 cup brown sugar
7 slices toast

Cook bacon until crisp. Remove from pan and add bell peppers and onions, which have been cut into small pieces, to bacon fat. Let simmer until done but not brown. To this add tomatoes, brown sugar, salt and pepper to taste. Let simmer until juice is almost gone. Break up toast and bacon into tomato mixture, place in a casserole, cover with toasted bread crumbs, one tablespoon brown sugar and dot with butter. Bake in a moderate oven for about 30 minutes. If a less rich dish is wanted, omit onions and bell peppers. (Serves 8 to 10)

PORK and BEAN CASSEROLE

1 clove garlic, minced
1 medium onion, chopped
3 tablespoons bacon drippings
2 cups pork and beans
2½ cups kidney beans
2½ cups green lima beans
½ cup catsup
3 tablespoons vinegar (apple cider)
2 tablespoons dark brown sugar
1 teaspoon dry mustard
1 teaspoon salt
½ teaspoon pepper

Saute garlic and onions in bacon drippings. Add all other ingredients and bake at 350 degrees for about 1 hour.

BAKED STUFFED TOMATOES

8 medium-sized tomatoes
1 green onion top (scallion), chopped
1 cup ground ham or ground beef
2 cups stale bread, softened in milk
1 egg, beaten
¼ stick margarine
Tony's Creole Seasoning or salt and pepper
Bread crumbs

Scoop inside pulp from tomatoes and turn upside down to drain. Fry onion to light brown in margarine, add pulp and ham or ground beef. Cook until nearly all water is out of tomatoes.

Squeeze out all surplus milk in bread and measure 1½ cups. Add to ham mixture, add egg and seasoning. Mix well and cook until rather dry. Stuff tomato shells with this dressing and sprinkle top with bread crumbs. Bake at 350 degrees for about 15 minutes. (Serves 8)

SMOTHERED OKRA and TOMATOES

2 pounds okra
3 tablespoons oil
1 tablespoon flour
1 medium onion, chopped
½ green bell pepper, chopped
2 medium sticks celery, chopped
5 fresh tomatoes or 1 large can
Tony's Creole Seasoning or salt and pepper

Wash okra, cut and fry in 2 tablespoons oil until it is not sticky (do not use black iron pot).

In another skillet make a medium dark roux with 1 tablespoon oil and 1 tablespoon flour. Add chopped onion, bell pepper and celery and simmer until wilted. Add tomatoes and simmer for 5 minutes. Add okra, season well with Tony's Creole Seasoning or salt and pepper, and turn fire down low. Cook for 1 hour. (Serves 6)

NOTE: Can be frozen for later use. Ideal for gumbos.

BROCCOLI CASSEROLE

1 large onion, chopped
½ stick margarine
3 packages chopped broccoli (from freezer case)
2 cups cream of mushroom soup
1½ packages garlic cheese
4-ounce can mushrooms
½ cup chopped, blanched almonds
½ cup bread crumbs

Saute onions in margarine and add drained broccoli, mushroom soup, cheese, mushrooms and ¼ cup almonds. Cook until cheese is completely melted. Season to taste and pour into a casserole. Sprinkle remaining almonds and bread crumbs on top. Bake in 300-degree oven until bubbly. (Serves 8)

TURNIP CASSEROLE

6 cups mashed turnips
8-ounce package cream cheese
¼ cup sugar
1 stick margarine
Bread crumbs, buttered

Salt and cook enough turnips to make six cups of mashed turnips. Drain and mash. Add softened cream cheese, sugar and margarine and mix well. Pour into casserole and top with bread crumbs. Bake in 350-degree oven until bubbly hot and lightly browned. (Serves 8 - 10)

NOTE: Rutabagas or carrots may also be used in this recipe. For a Christmas effect, pimento strips in the form of a poinsettia adds a nice effect on top of crumbs.

MARINATED GREEN BELL PEPPERS

Put peppers, one at a time, on a long fork or skewer. Hold over open flame, turning until blistered all over. Put each pepper into a paper bag, as blistered, and leave in closed bag for 15 minutes to steam. Remove, peel and marinate 4 hours in ½ olive oil and ½ wine vinegar mixture. Drain and serve.

TONY'S CRAWFISH STUFFED BELL PEPPERS

1 pound crawfish tails, peeled
2 cups Basic Vegetable Mix (see page 5)
6 medium bell peppers
½ stick margarine
2 eggs
1 cup bread crumbs
Tony's Creole Seasoning to taste

Melt margarine in aluminum skillet or Dutch oven (do not use black iron pot). Chop each crawfish tail into 4 pieces and season with Tony's Creole Seasoning. Add crawfish, eggs, Basic Vegetable Mix and saute at least 5 minutes. Remove from heat and add bread crumbs to thicken mixture.

Parboil cleaned bell peppers in salted water until soft. Fill with crawfish mixture, sprinkle tops with remaining bread crumbs. Place in casserole, cover bottom of dish with water to prevent sticking, and bake in 300-degree oven 30 to 40 minutes. (Serves 6)

STUFFED GREEN BELL PEPPERS

6 green bell peppers
6 cups cooked minced meat (chicken, lamb, veal, roast pork or shrimp)
1 onion, minced
1 tablespoon butter, melted
1 tablespoon parsley, minced
1 teaspoon salt
¼ cup bread crumbs or rice
1 egg, beaten
1 cup water or beef bouillon

Cut peppers in half, crosswise, remove seeds and cut off stems. Mix all remaining ingredients together, except water or bouillon. Fill peppers with mixture, stand in pan, and pour water around them. Bake in 350-degree oven, basting often, until tops are toasty brown. (Serves 6)

NOTE: Corn may be substituted for meat.

TONY'S CREAMED GARLIC SPINACH

2 10-ounce packages frozen spinach, leaf or chopped
1 tablespoon each, butter and olive oil
1 large onion, finely chopped
4 cloves garlic, mashed
2 tablespoons all purpose flour
¾ cup Half and Half cream
¼ teaspoon powdered nutmeg
1 cup freshly grated Parmesan cheese
Salt and pepper to taste

Follow directions for frozen spinach and set aside. Combine oil and butter in a wide frying pan and cook over medium heat. When butter is melted, add onions and garlic. Cook, stirring until onions are soft. Stir in flour, blending well. Remove from heat and blend in half and half cream and nutmeg. Add drained spinach and return to high heat, stirring until bubbly. Remove from heat and mix in ½ cup Parmesan cheese, salt and pepper. Sprinkle with remaining cheese and serve hot. You can substitute leeks, broccoli, cabbage or fresh asparagus.

SPINACH CASSEROLE LUCILLE

2 packages frozen chopped spinach
2 tablespoons flour
4 tablespoons margarine
2 tablespoons chopped onion
½ cup pure cream or milk
½ cup spinach liquid
Tony's Creole Seasoning to taste
1 roll jalapeno cheese (from dairy case)
1 teaspoon Worcestershire sauce
½ cup buttered bread crumbs

Cook spinach following directions on package. Drain and reserve liquid. Melt margarine in saucepan over low heat. Add flour, stirring until blended and smooth, but not brown. Add onion and cook until wilted.

Pour in spinach liquid and cream slowly, stirring constantly to avoid lumps. Cook until smooth and thick. Add seasoning and cheese, stir until melted. Combine with cooked spinach. Put into a casserole, top with bread crumbs and place in 350-degree oven until hot. (Serves 6)

CHICKEN ARTICHOKE CASSEROLE

SAUCE:

1 cup oleo
½ cup flour
3½ cups milk
½ tablespoon red pepper
1 tablespoon Accent
2 cloves garlic
½ pound "rat" cheese, cut up
3 ounces Gruyere cheese, cup up

Make cream sauce from above. Cook until it bubbles and cheese melts.

ADD:

Meat from 1 boiled chicken
2 large cans button mushrooms
2 large cans artichoke hearts

Put combined mixture in casserole and bake at 350 degrees for 30 minutes. You may substitute lobster, shrimp or crabmeat, or the three combined.

ASPARAGUS CREAM SAUCE CASSEROLE

1 No. 2 can green asparagus
2 tablespoons margarine
2 tablespoons flour
1 cup milk
¼ cup grated Cheddar cheese
½ cup chopped celery
1 teaspoon onion juice
½ teaspoon Worcestershire sauce
Salt and pepper to taste
3 eggs, hard-cooked and chopped
½ can pimentos, chopped
½ cup buttered bread crumbs

Make white sauce by melting margarine, adding flour, slowly adding milk and stirring constantly. Cook and stir slowly until sauce thickens. Add cheese, celery, onion juice, Worcestershire sauce, salt, pepper, eggs and pimentos to sauce. Drain asparagus and add to mixture.

Pour into casserole, top with bread crumbs. Bake in 350-degree oven for 15 to 20 minutes until hot and bread crumbs are brown. (Serves 6)

TUNA FISH CAULIFLOWER CASSEROLE

1 6¾-ounce can tuna, drained
1 lb. cauliflower, cooked
1½ cups peeled, diced potatoes
½ cup diced celery
2 tablespoons chopped onion
10½-ounce can cream of mushroom soup
¼ cup milk
Pinch of thyme
¾ tablespoon salt
Pieces of pimento
8-ounce can buttermilk biscuits

Wash cauliflower and cut stems into quater-inch slices. Cut large flowerets in half. Bring ¼ cup water to a boil and add cauliflower slices. Cover and cook 5 minutes. Add flowerets and cook about 5 minutes longer. Drain and put in the bottom of oiled 12x8-inch baking dish.

Meanwhile cook potatoes, celery, and onion in ½ cup boiling water until tender, about 10 minutes. Add mushroom soup, milk, thyme, salt and tuna. Gently blend all ingredients together. Pour over cauliflower and garnish with pimento. Top with biscuits.

Bake 15 to 20 minutes in 375-degree oven, or until biscuits are brown. (Serves 6)

CASSEROLE of STRING BEANS and CARROTS AU GRATIN

1 cup fresh string beans, boiled or canned
1 cup diced carrots, boiled
4 tablespoons butter
1½ cups milk
1 cup grated Velveeta cheese
3 tablespoons flour
2 egg yolks
2 talespoons grated onion
Tony's Creole Seasoning to taste

Make a sauce with melted butter, onion and a tablespoon of water. Cook until onion is transparent. Add the flour, stir in milk gradually, then add grated cheese to sauce. Melt the cheese by beating. Add egg yolks and mix well. Mix vegetables together in a casserole and pour sauce over them. Place diced bread crumbs on top and cook 30 minutes at 300 degrees. (Serves 4 to 6)

STEWED CORN

12 large tender ears of corn
3 medium size fresh tomatoes or 17-ounce can of whole tomatoes
1 cup minced onions
1 teaspoon sugar
2 tablespoons parsley
1 tablespoon green bell pepper, minced
2 tablespoons onion tops
½ pound salt meat, boiled to remove salt
⅔ cup cooking oil

Score the ears of corn down each row with knife, then cut from cob. With knife, press out all the pulp. Add chopped tomatoes and onions to corn.

After the meat has been boiled, fry to a golden brown. Add corn, onions and tomatoes. Let stew or saute for about 40 minutes, stirring frequently. Add 1½ cup of water, parsley, onion tops and bell pepper. Salt and pepper to taste. Cook about 30 more minutes. (Serves 8)

CREAMED ONIONS

12 small white onions
6 tablespoons margarine
8 level tablespoons flour
½ pound cheddar cheese, grated
2 cups milk
Tony's Creole Seasoning or salt and pepper
Salt
Paprika

Boil onions in salted water until fork-tender. Melt margarine over low heat, add flour and stir well until blended. Remove from heat, gradually stir in milk and return to heat. Cook, stirring constantly, until thick and smooth. Add onions, cheese and seasoning. When ready to serve, sprinkle with paprika. (Serves 4)

FRENCH FRIED ONIONS

½ cup milk
½ cup flour
1 teaspoon melted shortening
½ teaspoon salt
1 egg yolk
1 large white onion or more

Cut large onion across into slices about ½-inch thick. Separate slices into rings and set in ice water until cold. Remove rings from water and dry. Dip rings in a thin batter. Place in a frying basket and fry in deep shortening at 360 degrees until well browned. Drain and salt lightly before serving.

SMOTHERED CREOLE LEEKS

2 bunches leeks (about 10 medium size)
½ stick butter
2 eggs
¼ cup pure cream
½ teaspoon yellow food coloring
Tony's Creole Seasoning or salt and pepper

Cut off green tops of leeks and discard. Cut white bottoms in ½-inch slices and place in a saucepan. Season with Tony's Creole Seasoning or salt and pepper and add just enough water to cover the leeks. Cover and simmer until leeks are very tender and all water is absorbed. Mash leeks and add butter.

Remove from fire. Beat eggs, pour in cream and add to leek mixture. Mix well. Color with food color to enhance looks. Serve hot. (Serves 4)

CHEESE and ONION PIE

½ pound Swiss cheese, grated
1 large onion, sliced
1 10-inch pie crust
2 eggs, beaten lightly
2 tablespoons flour
1 cup heavy cream
1 cup milk
½ teaspoon curry powder
¼ teaspoon ground nutmeg
2 dashes Tabasco sauce
1 teaspoon salt
Freshly ground black pepper

Place pie crust in 10-inch pie plate. Mix cheese thoroughly with flour and spread in bottom of crust. Separate onion slices into rings and arrange rings on cheese mixture. Make a mixture of eggs, cream, milk, curry powder, nutmeg, Tabasco, salt and pepper. Pour egg mixture over cheese and onion rings. Bake in 350-degree oven for 45 minutes. (Serves 6)

BRABANT POTATOES

6 Irish potatoes, medium
1 large onion
1 stick margarine
Tony's Creole Seasoning

Cut boiled and peeled potatoes into 8 pieces. Slice onion in thin rounds. Melt margarine in Dutch oven and fry onion and potatoes, turning often until brown. Season with Tony's Creole Seasoning or salt and pepper. (Serves 4)

IRISH POTATO CASSEROLE

6 medium-sized Irish potatoes
2 large onions, thinly sliced in rounds
½ pound sharp Cheddar cheese grated or cut in pieces
2 10½-ounce size, cans mushroom soup
Salt and pepper to taste
1 pint milk
Paprika

Boil potatoes until nearly done and drain. Peel and slice in thin rounds. Place in greased casserole in layers — layer of potatoes, layer of onion rounds, layer of cheese. Season with salt and pepper. Cover with mixture of mushroom soup and milk, then repeat layers and seasoning until completed.

Garnish with paprika, place in 300-degree oven and bake until cheese is well melted and bubbly. Good! (Serves 6)

JOHNNY MAZETTE

(Very Good)

1 pound ground beef
1 pound ground pork
1 pound noodles
2 cups grated American cheese (½ pound)
1 can mushroom soup
1 can tomato sauce
1 can (10½ ounce) condensed tomato soup
1 can (4-ounce) sliced mushrooms, with liquid
½ cup chopped stuffed olives
2 cups chopped green pepper
1 cup chopped celery
2 cups chopped onions
1 cup butter or oleo
2 teaspoons salt

In a very large skillet, saute pepper, celery, onions and ground meat in very hot butter. Add salt. Reduce heat, cook 5 minutes. Stir in mushrooms and canned liquid soup and sauces. Cook 5 minutes.

Cook noodles, following box directions; drain. Turn noodles into a 14 x 10 x 2½ inch roasting pan. Add sauce mixture and gently stir until well mixed. Add grated cheese on top. Bake at 350 degrees for 35 minutes. (Yields 12 generous portions)

SQUASH CASSEROLE

5 to 6 pounds white squash
1 stick butter or oleo
2 medium onions
2 medium bell peppers
1 cup celery
1 small jar pimento, cut
1 cup cracker crumbs
4 eggs, beaten
2 slices bacon, fried and crumbled
Several drops Tabasco
Salt and pepper to taste

Wash squash and cut into quarters. Peel, remove seeds, cut squash into small pieces. Cook in boiling, salted water until tender. In the meantime, saute onions, bell peppers and celery in butter or oleo. Drain cooked squash, mash and add to skillet of sauted vegetables. Cook a few minutes, stirring constantly. Save bacon, add remaining ingredients and cook a little longer. Pour into shallow Pyrex dish, dot with small pieces of bacon (seasoned bread crumbs may be also added) and bake at 350 degrees, 20 to 30 minutes. (Serves 8 to 10 people)

ZUCCHINI SQUASH with DILL SAUCE

2 pounds Zucchini, peeled, seeded and cut into Julienne strips 1/8-inch wide and 3 inches long
1/2 teaspoon salt
2 tablespoons butter
2 tablespoons flour
1 cup sour cream
1 teaspoon sugar
2 teaspoons vinegar
1 tablespoon finely chopped fresh dill

Season the Zucchini with salt in a mixing bowl. Let it stand for 1/2 hour, then spread the strips on paper towels and pat dry. Melt butter in a 1 1/2-quart saucepan. When hot, add the Zucchini.

Toss it about in butter with a spoon until well coated, then cover the pan. Turn heat low and simmer 10 minutes or until barely tender. Don't overcook.

Beat flour into the sour cream with a wire whisk. Pour mixture over the Zucchini and stirring gently, simmer 2 or 3 minutes, until the sauce is thick and smooth. Stir in sugar, vinegar and dill and season to taste. (Serves 6)

CUCUMBERS STUFFED with HAM and SOUR PICKLES

2 garden fresh cucumbers, 6 to 8 inches long
½ teaspoon salt
2 sardines (boneless)
¼ pound boiled ham, diced in ¼ inch chunks
2 hard-boiled eggs, coarsely chopped
2 teaspons finely chopped onions
2 tablespoons minced sour pickles
1 teaspoon prepared mustard
2 to 4 tablespoons mayonnaise, freshly made

Cut ½-inch off the top of each cucumber, then peel the cucumbers with vegetable scraper or knife. Cut out the seeds and center pulp with a long iced teaspoon, leaving shell about ¼-inch thick. Pour ¼ teaspoon salt into each cucumber, rubbing it in evenly with your forefinger. Let the shells stand 15 minutes, then dry them inside with a paper towel.

In a medium-sized mixing bowl, mash the sardines into a paste with a wooden spoon. Add the ham, eggs, onions, pickles, mustard and 2 tablespoons mayonnaise. Stir ingredients together until mixture holds its shape with a spoon. If too dry, add more mayonnaise.

Stuff cucumbers by standing them on end and spooning the filling in, tamping down with a spoon as you proceed. When cucumbers are tightly packed, wrap them separately in aluminum foil and refrigerate for 2 hours or until filling is firm.

To serve, slice cucumbers crosswise, or on a slant, in slices about ½-inch thick. (Serve as Hors d'oeuvres).

STUFFED COOKED CUCUMBERS

6 large cucumbers (about 6 inches long)
1 pound ground meat
1 stick margarine
1 onion, chopped
½ bell pepper, chopped
2 sticks celery, chopped
2 cloves garlic, chopped
1 cup bread crumbs
1 egg
Tony's Creole Seasoning or salt and pepper

Fry the meat with margarine in skillet until brown. Chop the vegetables and saute with meat. Add bread crumbs, egg and mix well. Cook for 5 minutes.

In separate baking pan, parboil cucumbers and pour off water. Cut opening lengthwise of cucumber and remove pulp and seeds. Add to meat mixture. Stuff cavities with meat mixture and sprinkle with bread crumbs. Place in greased baking pan with a little water and cook for 20 minutes in 300-degree oven. (Serves 6)

NEW ORLEANS RED BEANS and RICE

1 pound dried red beans, soaked overnight
½ pound pickled pork, cut in strips
1 onion, chopped fine
½ green bell pepper, chopped
Tony's Creole Seasoning or salt and pepper

Combine all ingredients with enough water to cover well and cook until beans are tender. Add water from time to time to make a thick, rich gravy. Serve with cooked rice.

NOTE: 2 large cans of red beans may be used in place of the cooked dried beans. (Serves 6)

HERE'S ANOTHER TIP

Are You Watching Your Weight

And Does Everything You Eat

Taste Bland? Then Try

Tony Chachere's Famous

Creole Seasoning.

It Makes Everything Taste

Better

EGGS
GRITS
PANCAKES

TONY CHACHERE'S CREOLE STEAK SAUCE

For Steaks, Hamburgers, Ground Beef, Roast, Poultry and Fish!

HOW to FRY an EGG

To get the full flavor and tenderness of a fried egg, never get the frying pan too hot.

Heat heavy pan on low heat until margarine or bacon fat is melted (if you prefer, use cooking oil). Use just enough to cover bottom of pan. Add egg; cook slowly until white is firm. If yolk is basted with a little fat the top will be white. If desired, egg can be turned during frying.

ANOTHER WAY to COOK EGGS

Use skillet with tightly-fitting lid. Melt butter in skillet until it starts to brown. Break eggs in bowl, add 2 tablespoons milk to each egg and pour in skillet. Put on lid and simmer until desired doneness. Remove with egg turner to warmed plate. Serve with 1 drop Tabasco sauce on each yolk and salt and pepper.

HEAVENLY EGGS

8 eggs
1 small onion, chopped fine
3 tablespoons butter or margarine
¼ cup milk or pure cream
¼ bell pepper, chopped fine
1 piece bacon, crumbled

Saute onions, bell pepper in butter until soft. Add beaten eggs and bacon in milk and cook until moisture is nearly evaporated. Season with salt and black pepper and serve. You may also add your choice of shrimp, mushrooms, crab meat, etc., but be sure to saute them in the butter with the onions and bell pepper. (Serves 4)

SCRAMBLED EGGS with GREEN PEPPERS

1 green bell pepper, chopped fine
1 small onion, minced
½ stick margarine
4 eggs, well beaten
2 tablespoons cream
Salt and pepper to taste

Melt margarine in skillet and fry bell pepper and onion until tender. Add eggs mixed with cream, seasoning to taste, and stir slowly until done. (Serves 2)

HAM and EGGS JAMBALAYA

2 cups boiled rice
4 eggs
1 slice ham, cut up
½ onion, cut up
½ stick margarine

Melt margarine. Cook ham and onions in margarine until onions are wilted. Add cooked rice until hot. Add eggs, mix well and stir thoroughly. Salt and black pepper. (Serves 4)

EGGS FLORENTINE

4 tablespoons butter
4 tablespoons all-purpose flour
2 (10-ounce) packages frozen chopped spinach
2 cups light cream
8 eggs
4 ounces mozzarella cheese, grated
½ teaspoon grated nutmeg
2 teaspoons grated Parmesan cheese
1 teaspoon Worcestershire
¼ teaspoon Tabasco
¼ teaspoon dry mustard
Salt and pepper to taste

Cook chopped spinach and drain thoroughly. Put light cream in a saucepan and combine mozzarella cheese (or other) with it. Place over low heat until cheese is melted. Season with nutmeg, salt and pepper, Worcestershire and mustard. Taste for seasoning, adding more if needed. In a little bowl, rub flour into butter, add Tabasco, stir in spinach and heat gently.
Spread this mixture into bottom of 4 individual greased baking dishes or casseroles. On top of each spinach bed, break 2 eggs. Sprinkle each with Parmesan cheese and bake in a moderate oven, 350 degrees, about 15 minutes or until the eggs are set. (Serves 4)

EGGS BENEDICT

4 eggs
1 large tomato (quartered)
4 hamburger buns
4 slices ham, cut in circle to fit bun
½ stick margarine
1 cup Hollandaise sauce (hot)
Salt and pepper to taste

Poach the eggs, broil ham and tomato slices, toast and butter the buns. Put ham and tomato on bun and poached egg on top. Season with salt and pepper. Cover with Hollandaise and bun top. Serve hot. (Serves 4)

FRANK'S SPANISH OMELETTE

1 stick margarine
1 can tomato sauce
¼ cup milk
½ onion, minced
8 eggs, well beaten
1 No. 1 can sifted petit pois (green peas), drained
Tony's Creole Seasoning or salt and pepper to taste
Parmesan cheese, grated

In skillet melt ½ stick margarine, add onion and saute. Add tomato sauce and cook about 10 minutes.

In a separate skillet (deep) melt ½ stick margarine; add eggs, milk and petit pois. Season with Tony's Creole Seasoning or salt and pepper. Cook until almost done and pour tomato sauce over all. Continue cooking until eggs are done. Sprinkle top with Parmesan cheese. (Serves 4)

TONY'S CRABMEAT OMELETTE

¼ pound lump crab meat
2 whole stalks green onion tops (scallions), chopped fine
2 tablespoons pure cream or milk
4 eggs (large)
½ stick butter or oleo
Tony's Creole Seasoning to taste

Saute chopped onion tops and crab meat in melted butter. Mix cream with eggs, beat and add to crabmeat mixture. Mix gently. Do not have fire too hot, just enough to cook eggs. While still soft, serve. You can substitute crawfish, shrimp or lobster. (Serves 2)

SHIRRED EGGS

6 eggs
2 slices bacon
¼ stick margarine
6 tablespoons heavy cream
Salt and black pepper to taste
Pinch of dry mustard

Cut bacon into 6 pieces, saute until crisp. Drain and save bacon, discard bacon fat. Add mustard to cream and stir well. Put 1 tablespoon cream into 6 individual china baking dishes and break 1 egg on top of the cream; season to taste. Put 1 piece of bacon on top of each egg and cover baking dishes. Bake in moderate oven, 375 degrees, for 10 minutes or until eggs are set. Remove and serve. (Serves 6)

NOTE: Custard cups, covered with foil, may be used instead of china baking dishes.

TONY'S HEAVENLY PANCAKES

1 cup all-purpose flour
¾ cup Half & Half cream
1 tablespoon sugar
2 tablespoons melted butter
2 eggs, well beaten
2 teaspoons baking powder
½ teaspoon salt

Mix flour, baking powder, sugar and salt. Add melted butter and beaten eggs to half & half cream. Mix well. Add dry ingredients and stir just enough to get an even mixture. If too thick, add some more half & half cream so that batter pours easily. Use tablespoon batter dropped onto hot greased griddle. When brown, turn over and brown other side. Serve with butter and fig preserves and a glass of milk. Man that's living! Enough for one big man or a regular couple.

CORN MEAL BATTER CAKES

1 cup corn meal
1 tablespoon flour
1 egg
1 teaspoon salt
Milk to make batter very thin

Scald corn meal with enough boiling water to dampen well. When cool sift in flour and salt. Add beaten egg and milk to make thin batter. Beat well. Have griddle very hot and well greased. This makes a cake with a nice crispy edge. Use no baking powder. (Serves 2)

POTATO PANCAKES

7 or 8 medium Idaho potatoes
1 large onion
1 tablespoon salt
1 teaspoon black pepper
2 eggs
2 tablespoons flour

Grate onions and potatoes. Put in a colander and mash out the juice. Let juice stand and settle. Pour off liquid and return starch to mixture. Separate the eggs and add yolks to the mixture and other ingredients. Beat egg whites until fluffy and fold in. Drop by spoonfuls, on a greased griddle, turning when brown. (Serves 8)

CREOLE GARLIC GRITS for BREAKFAST

1 cup 5-minute grits
4 cups water
6 strips bacon
4 cloves garlic, minced
1 stick margarine
8 eggs
Salt and pepper to taste

Cook grits, seasoned with 1 teaspoon salt, for 5 minutes; add minced garlic and stir. Fry bacon slices until crisp and crumble well on small plate. Fry eggs in ½ stick margarine, your choice, over or up.

Place one-fourth of grits in center of serving plate and add pat of margarine. Sprinkle with crumbled bacon and top with two eggs. Season to taste. Serve with hot biscuits. (Serves 4)

JIM BOWIE'S HUSH PUPPIES

2 cups corn meal
1 cup flour
2 tablespoons minced onions
1 egg
2 tablespoons bacon drippings
Tony's Creole Seasoning to taste
2 tablespoons baking powder
Milk
Deep fat for frying

Mix all ingredients with just enough milk to make a thick mixture. Wet hands and roll mixture into 1½-inch balls. Drop into deep fat and remove when brown. Drain on absorbent paper.

JIM BOWIE'S COUCHE — COUCHE et CAILLE

2 cups corn meal
1 teaspoon salt
1 teaspoon baking powder
1½ cups milk
½ cup pan drippings or margarine
Clabber (curdled milk)

Thoroughly mix corn meal, baking powder, salt and milk. In a heavy skillet heat pan drippings and add mixture. Stir and lower heat; cover and cook 15 minutes, stirring often. When a crust is formed on bottom, stir and serve in cereal bowls and cover with clabber.

BREADS

TONY'S HOT TAMALES

Ingredients for Masa

2 lbs. corn flour (Masa)
½ lb. pork lard or shortening
2 cups of drained broth from meat
1 bag corn husks or oiled papers
3 level tablespoonfuls Tony Chachere Famous Creole Seasoning or salt and pepper

Ingredients for Meat

2 lbs. coarse ground beef
2 lbs. coarse ground lean pork
1½ oz. chili powder (3 tablespoons) fresh
1 teaspoon paprika
1 level tablespoon Tony Chachere Famous Creole Seasoning or salt and pepper
½ teaspoon comino (cumin powder)

Place corn husks in hot water for 15 minutes. Combine chili powder, paprika, 1 tablespoon Tony Chachere's Famous Creole Seasoning and comino in 1 cup of water in blender and blend for 5 seconds. In large sauce pan place meat and add 5 - 8 oz. cups of water and ingredients from blender and cook over medium heat for approx. 30 minutes or until brown. Stirring occasionally, add a dash of shortening if you wish.

Place Masa in large bowl, add ½ lb. shortening, 3 level tablespoonfuls Tony Chachere Famous Creole Seasoning or salt and pepper and 2 cups of drained broth from meat. Mix well by hand. Remove corn husks from water and separate them carefully. Spread Masa on corn husks (thin). After spreading Masa on corn husks fill each one with approx. 1 full tablespoon of meat in the center and roll flat folding the long end and sealing the other.

In Dutch oven, place remaining corn husks at bottom of some kind of drain tray with 2 cups of water. If you have a bottom drain tray for your Dutch oven use it and place remaining husks on top of the tamales. Arrange tamales pinwheel like inside pot and cook for approx. 1½ hours over medium heat. Makes 6 dozen tamales.

Variations

Use same ingredients and instructions for making 6 different kinds of tamales. Those included are:

1. Ground pork
2. Ground pork and venison
3. Ground beef and ground pork
4. Ground beef, ground pork and venison
5. Beans (mashed or refried) any kind
6. Hogs head (boiled, boned, cook and grind)

HARD CRUST FRENCH BREAD

2½ cups warm water
1 package dry yeast or
1 yeast cake
2 tablespoons sugar
1 teaspoon salt
7 cups flour
2 egg whites, well beaten

In large bowl combine yeast, warm water, sugar and salt; stir until dissolved. Gradually add sifted flour and mix until well blended. Knead 10 minutes on well-floured surface until dough is smooth and satiny. Let rise in warm place until doubled in bulk. Punch down and place on floured surface. Knead 3 or 4 times to remove air and divide into 4 equal pieces.

Shape into loaves, place in well-greased pans. Slash tops and brush with egg whites. Let rise until double in bulk and bake 15 minutes in pre-heated 450-degree oven or 30 minutes at 350 degrees. Remove from pans and cool. (Makes 4 loaves)

NOTE: Wrap extra loaves in aluminum foil and freeze. To reserve, warm in foil 20 minutes at 350 degrees.

HOMEMADE BREAD

(Makes 6 1¼-pound loaves)

Baking pans about
5½" x 3½" x 2½" high
8 cups all-purpose flour
3 packages dry yeast
2 tablespoons salt
⅔ cup sugar
⅔ cup salad oil (Wesson)
1 quart and 1 cup
lukewarm water

Pour warm water, about 90 degrees (lukewarm) into a large, warm mixing bowl. Put in dry yeast. Let set until yeast is dissolved (5 to 10 minutes). Add salt, sugar, salad oil and stir. Add 4 cups flour, stir well. Add 4 more cups flour, stir again. Add 1 cup flour at a time and knead well until dough can be held on hand extended.

Knead on board or in the bowl. Put in a bowl to rise and cover top to prevent drying. Dough should rise 2 or 2½ times original size. Work down to original size. Make into loaves.

Roll into oiled pans (2 tablespoons oil in each pan). Let rise (at 80 degrees) to 2 to 2½ times original size, about 1½ to 2 hours. Can be put in a cold or preheated oven.

Bake 30 minutes at 250 degrees, then raise temperature to 340 degrees and bake until brown. When baked, remove from pans and cool on a rack.

DILLY CASSEROLE BREAD

1 package yeast
¼ cup warm water
1 egg, beaten
2 tablespoons sugar
1 tablespoon minced onion
1 tablespoon margarine, melted
2 teaspoons dill seed
1 teaspoon salt
¼ teaspoon soda
1 cup lukewarm cottage cheese
2½ cups flour

Dissolve yeast in warm water. Pour cottage cheese in small bowl, set in pan of water to warm. Combine egg, sugar, onion, butter, dill seed, salt, soda with the warmed cottage cheese. Add yeast mixture and stir well. Gradually add sifted flour to make a stiff dough and beat well with spoon. Mixture will not be stiff enough to knead. Place in warm place and let rise until double in bulk, then stir down.

Pour in greased 8-inch casserole and let rise again. Bake at 350 degrees for 40 to 50 minutes until brown. Brush all over with butter. (Makes 1 loaf)

GRATED YAM BREAD

3 cups grated raw sweet potatoes
½ cup sugar
½ cup cane syrup
1 cup milk
1 teaspoon nutmeg
1 teaspoon cinnamon
2 tablespoons margarine, melted
½ cup chopped nuts
½ teaspoon salt
2 eggs, well beaten

In a large bowl, combine all ingredients except eggs. In another bowl beat eggs well and add to mixture. Blend and pour into a buttered, shallow baking pan. Bake in moderately hot oven, 375 degrees,for 50 to 60 minutes. (Serves 6)

GARLIC BREAD

1 loaf French bread
1 clove garlic
½ stick margarine, melted
4 tablespoons minced parsley
Parmesan cheese, grated
Paprika

Rub entire outside of French bread with garlic clove. Slice loaf lengthwise, down the middle, and cover with margarine. Sprinkle with Parmesan cheese and parsley; then sprinkle lightly with paprika. Place slices in a hot oven until crisp.

JIM BOWIE HOECAKES

1 teaspoon shortening, melted
2 cups flour
1 teaspoon salt
Boiling water sufficient to make batter

Mix all ingredients to make a dough. Flatten out on a floured board. Place near hot coals until browned and done or place in pie pan (or on cookie sheet) and cook in 400-degree oven until brown.

NOTE: These cakes may be baked on a griddle, as you would a griddle cake, and served with Louisiana cane syrup, butter and milk. But the old-timers, like Jim Bowie, always baked them on a hoe on hot coals in front of a wood fire; hence the name "hoe" cakes. The term "hoecake" is extensively used by the Cajuns of Louisiana.

PAIN PERDU

(Lost Bread)

2 eggs
1 cup milk
1 cup sugar
1 tablespoon cornstarch
½ teaspoon nutmeg
Sliced white bread, stale
Margarine or cooking oil
Powdered sugar

Beat eggs well; add sugar rapidly and continue to beat. Add cornstarch and, when well mixed, add milk and nutmeg. Dip bread slice in mixture, coating each side thoroughly. Use just enough margarine or oil to cover bottom of skillet and fry over moderate heat. Fry each side of slice until golden brown. Serve hot, sprinkled with powdered sugar.

GOLDEN SNACK BREAD

2 packages dry yeast (active)
1 cup warm water
4 to 4½ cups all-purpose flour
1 cup pasteurized process cheese spread (8-ounce jar)
2 tablespoons sugar
2 tablespoons soft butter
1 teaspoon salt

Soften yeast in warm water in large mixing bowl. Add 2 cups flour, cheese spread, sugar, butter and salt. Beat 2 minutes at medium mixer speed. Gradually add remaining flour. Mix thoroughly, cover. Let rise in warm place until light and doubled in size, about 30 minutes.

Prepare filling of your choice: jelly, preserves, peanut butter, etc. Roll out dough, half at a time, on floured surface to a 16 x 11 inch rectangle. Spread each with half of filling. Starting with the 16-inch side, roll up jelly roll fashion then seal edges and ends. Place diagonally, seam side down, on greased cookie sheets.

Using knife or scissors make a lengthwise cut from center halfway through loaf. Cover. Let rise in warm place until light, about 45 minutes. Bake at 350 degrees for 30 to 35 minutes.

AUNT LULU'S GRIT BREAD

Select 6 ears of corn just beyond the milk stage. Grit kernels by slicing three times to yield 2½ cups scraped corn kernels. To the kernels add the following:

1 cup sifted flour
2 teaspoons sugar
1¼ teaspoons salt
2½ teaspoons baking powder
1 egg, well-beaten
¼ cup melted butter

To the flour add sugar, salt and baking powder; sift together over the gritted corn, mixing thoroughly. Stir in egg alternately with melted butter. No liquid is necessary as moisture is given by the gritten corn. Put into greased shallow pan and bake at 425 degrees for 30 to 35 minutes. Serve hot with generous slabs of country butter.

HOT MEXICAN CORNBREAD

1 cup yellow cornmeal
1 cup sweet milk with
½ teaspoon soda
1 teaspoon salt
2 jalapeno peppers, chopped fine
1 can corn, cream style
2 eggs, well beaten
1 cup green onions, minced (scallions)
½ pound Cheddar cheese, grated
¼ cup cooking oil

Mix together all ingredients, except the oil, and reserve half the cheese for topping. Put oil in skillet and heat until hot. Pour over cornmeal mixture in bowl. Stir fast to melt cheese. Pour mixture into hot skillet and top with remaining cheese. Bake at 350 degrees for 40 minutes. (Serves 6 to 8)

SPOON BREAD

1½ cups boiling water
2 tablespoons melted butter
1 cup cornmeal
3 teaspoons baking powder
½ teaspoon salt
3 eggs
1 cup milk

Pour boiling water and butter over cornmeal and mix well. Allow to cool. Add baking powder, salt, well-beaten eggs and milk. Stir well and pour into a well-buttered baking dish. Bake in a 350-degree oven 40 minutes. (Serves 6)

BREAD DUMPLINGS

4 tablespoons butter
3 cups bread, cut in ½-inch cubes
3 tablespoons finely chopped onions
10 tablespoons flour
2 tablespoons finely chopped parsley
½ teaspoon salt
⅛ teaspoon nutmeg
¼ cup milk

Melt 3 tablespoons butter in a heavy skillet. When the foam subsides, add bread cubes. Toss them in butter until they are brown on all sides, then set aside.

Add the remaiing butter to the skillet and when it has melted, stir in the onions. Cook 3 or 4 minutes until they are lightly colored, then scrape them into a large mixing bowl. Stir in the flour, parsley, salt and nutmeg, and moisten with the milk. Knead lightly to form a dough. Gently fold in bread cubes and let the mixture stand for 30 minutes. Divide dough in half, and with your hands, knead and form into 2 long rolls about 2 inches in diameter.

Carefully place rolls in an 8-inch sauce pan half-full of boiling water. Cook gently over medium heat for 20 to 25 minutes, turning them once with a large spoon. Remove to paper towels to drain. Cut rolls in ½-inch slices while still hot.

Serve immediately with roast goose, chicken or any meat dish that has a gravy or sauce. (Makes about 12 dumplings)

BEER MUFFINS

4 cups Bisquick
3 tablespoons sugar
12-ounce can beer

Mix thoroughly and pour into greased muffin tin (half-full). Bake approximately 20 minutes at 350 degrees. (Makes 16)

TONY'S OLE-FASHIONED CREOLE CORN BREAD

2 cups yellow cornmeal
1 cup all-purpose flour
1 cup sour cream (from the dairy case)
3 tablespoons baking powder
2 eggs
1 cup cream style corn
1½ teaspoons salt (to taste)
½ cup bacon fat
Milk

Mix all ingredients together until well blended. Add enough milk to make the mixture pour easily. Place in greased muffin tins or baking pan. Place in preheated 400-degree oven until golden brown, about 20 to 30 minutes. Serve with butter and pure cane syrup (made in open kettle). Now you can sop your way to the Promised Land!

TONY'S

(Way back yonder when everybody made their own)

BISCUITS

5 cups self-rising flour (remember those 24-lb. sacks?)
½ cup bacon drippings
⅓ cup sugar (optional)
2 packages yeast
1 teaspoon soda
2 cups buttermilk (If you don't churn your own butter anymore, use store boughten.)

Sift flour, soda and sugar together. Add shortening and blend. Dissolve yeast in ¼ cup warm water and add with buttermilk to mixture. Mix well. Place on floured cutting board, cut into biscuits, place on greased baking sheets. Bake in preheated 400-degree oven until brown.

Makes a heap of biscuits. If too much, store in refrigerator and use as needed.

ROUGHNECK HOT ROLLS (18 rolls)

Recipes by Uncle Cotton (W.T.) Palmer, Offshore cook

1 cup warm water
½ cup sugar
2 (½-ounce) packs dry yeast
¾ cup shortening
6 cups plain flour
1½ tablespoons salt

Add warm water to mixing bowl. Add sugar to warm water, then add 2 packs of yeast and let stand. Let yeast come to top of water, then add shortening. Next add flour, then salt, mix well and place in greased mixing bowl. Let dough rise to twice the original size, then roll out on floured board to ¾-inch thickness. Cut rolls and place in greased pan and let rise. Bake at 400 degrees for 20 minutes or until brown. Butter tops and serve.

LAGNIAPPE POPOVER

2 cups self-rising flour
3 tablespoons mayonnaise
1 cup milk
1 teaspoon sugar

Combine all ingredients in a small bowl and mix thoroughly. Spoon into well-greased muffin tin and bake in a preheated 350-degree oven about 20 minutes. Yield: 1 dozen large muffins or 2 dozen small muffins.

Your kids will nag you to death for more.

JEANNINE'S PUMPKIN MUFFINS

1 cup mashed pumpkin
2 cups sugar
1½ cups Wesson oil
1 cup raisins
4 eggs
3 cups self-rising flour
1 teaspoon cinnamon
1 cup nuts chopped large

Rinse raisins and nuts in boiling water. Mix all ingredients together and bake in greased muffin pans at 350 degrees for 15 or 20 minutes.

Batter may be refrigerated and used as needed. My daughter, Jeannine, thinks this recipe is the greatest.

SWEETS

OFFSHORE PIE DOUGH
(3 pies)

Recipes by Uncle Cotton (W.T.) Palmer, Offshore cook

14 ounce plain flour (1 3/4 cups)
1/2 lb. shortening (1 cup)
1/2 tablespoon salt
1/2 teaspoon vinegar
1/2 cup cold water

Mix flour, shortening, salt and vinegar in a mixing bowl. Add 1/2 cup of cold water and stir well. Divide the dough into 3 equal parts and roll to desired thickness. Place in pie pans and bake at 380 degrees for 6 to 8 minutes or until golden brown.

COCONUT ROUSTABOUT COOKIES
(4 dozen)

Recipes by Uncle Cotton (W.T.) Palmer, Offshore cook

3 cups plain flour
1 cup shortening
1/2 tablespoon salt
1/2 tablespoon vanilla flavoring
1/2 teaspoon soda
1 cup sugar
2 cups coconut
2 cups oatmeal
2 cups mixed nuts
2 tablespoons baking powder
Add enough water to roll out easy

Mix all ingredients in a mixing bowl, stir well, then roll out on a floured board to 1/4-inch thickness. Cut out cookies with cutter then bake at 450 degrees for 8 to 10 minutes.

LAGNIAPPE BUTTERMILK PIE

1 9-inch unbaked pie crust
1¼ cups sugar
2 tablespoons cornstarch
3 eggs
½ teaspoon soda
½ teaspoon salt
⅓ cup melted butter or margarine
¼ cup lemon juice
1 cup buttermilk

Beat eggs, add sugar, cornstarch and salt, and beat one minute. Add remaining ingredients, mix well. Pour into unbaked pie shell and bake at 400 degrees for 10 minutes. Lower oven to 350 degrees and continue baking for 20-30 minutes until firm. (Serves 6 to 8)

OPELOUSAS PRALINES

2 cups sugar
Pinch salt
1 small can evaporated milk
2 tablespoons sugar (heaping)
2 teaspoons vanilla
3 cups shelled pecans

In one pot, put 2 cups sugar, salt and milk. Cook to softball stage (test by dropping a little in water or use candy thermometer). Remove from fire.

While this is cooking, caramelize (until brown) 2 heaping tablespoons sugar in a small, thick skillet. Combine with above mixture after it reaches test stage and take off fire. Add vanilla pecans and beat. Before candy crystallizes, dip out by separate spoonfuls and place on waxed paper to cool.

If mixture should crystallize too soon (before removing from pot) add a tablespoon of boiling water and beat again.

CREOLE BENNE PRALINES

2 cups fresh sesame seed
½ stick margarine
½ cup milk
2 cups sugar
2 teaspoons corn syrup
1 pinch salt

Stir sesame seeds in a dry Dutch oven or skillet, over medium heat, until parched light brown. In a saucepan heat milk, margarine, sugar, salt and syrup. Stir until thick; add parched seeds and stir until well mixed together. Pour mixture into pancake-size portions on well-greased cookie sheet and let cool.

NOTE: One hundred years ago this was a big treat for the children.

CREAMY SMOOTH PECAN PRALINES

2 cups sugar
½ cup white Karo syrup
½ cup water
2 cups pecan halves
½ stick margarine
1 tablespoon vanilla

Combine sugar, syrup, water and pecans in a heavy three-quart saucepan. Stir over medium heat until sugar is dissolved and mixture comes to a boil. Cook, stirring occasionally, until mixture reaches soft ball stage (small amount forms soft ball when dropped into cold water). Remove saucepan from heat, add margarine and vanilla.

Allow candy to cool. Whip until mixture gradually changes to lighter color and becomes creamy. Drop by tablespoonful on buttered cookie sheet. Push mixture from tablespoon with a teaspoon to hasten dropping before praline becomes too firm to shape.

PECAN PIE

3 eggs
½ cup sugar
1 cup white or dark Karo syrup
1 teaspoon vanilla extract
1 cup chopped nuts
½ teaspoon salt

Beat eggs slightly, add sugar, Karo, extract, nuts and salt. Beat well after each addition. Pour into unbaked 9-inch pie shell and bake at 325 degrees for 50 minutes or until brown. For miniature pies, place pie dough in muffin pan, fill with mixture and bake same as above.

RITZ PIE

3 egg whites, well beaten
1 cup sugar
½ teaspoon baking powder
23 Ritz crackers, rolled fine
1 cup pecans, chopped
1 teaspoon vanilla extract

Mix all above ingredients into pie plate and bake 25 to 30 minutes at 350 degrees. Use Cool Whip over it when cool.

DATE TORTE

1 cup dates, in halves
1 cup walnuts, in fours
1 cup granulated sugar
2 eggs, beat separately
2 tablespoons flour
1 teaspoon vanilla

Cream eggs and sugar, add fruit and nuts, then white of eggs gradually, then flour and vanilla. Bake in moderate oven, 350 degrees, from 30 to 45 minutes.

CHERRIES JUBILEE

1 pint jar or 1 can pitted Bing cherries
½ teaspoon arrowroot or cornstarch
2 ounces Kirsch

Pour the juice from cherries into the top pan or blazer of a chafing dish. Place the pan directly over the flame and bring juice to a boil. Thicken juice with arrowroot or starch dissolved in a little water, and then add cherries. Stir mixture until heated through. Pour Kirsch over cherries and blaze.

NOTE: Serve the flaming cherries and sauce over vanilla ice cream or alone.

FRENCH CHOCOLATE CUP

(Pot de Creme)

2 cups pure cream
6 ounces grated sweet, cooking chocolate
2 tablespoons sugar
6 egg yolks
1 teaspoon vanilla
Whipped cream, for topping

In a heavy saucepan combine cream, chocolate and sugar. Stir over low heat until chocolate melts and cream is scalded. Remove from heat. Beat egg yolks in a bowl and pour a little of the hot mixture on yolks; blend well. Return to remaining hot mixture, add vanilla, mix well. Strain into custard cups and cover with foil.

Set in pan of warm water and bake at 300 degrees for 20 minutes. Chill in refrigerator. When ready to serve, top with whipped cream. (Serves 6)

BAKED ALASKA

2 tablespoons margarine
4 egg whites
Pinch salt
¼ cup sugar
4 egg yolks
½ teaspoon vanilla
½ cup all-purpose flour
1 cup orange marmalade or apricot preserves
1 or 2 tablespoons orange juice
1 quart vanilla ice cream, slightly softened

Brush a tablespoon of soft margarine over the bottom and sides of an 11- x 16-inch jelly roll pan. Line pan with a 22-inch strip of waxed paper, letting extra paper extend over ends of pan. Brush remaining margarine over the paper and scatter a small handful of flour over it. Tip pan from side to side to spread flour evenly. Then turn pan over and rap it sharply to dislodge the excess flour. Preheat oven to 400 degrees.

In a mixing bowl beat the egg whites and salt until it forms soft waving peaks. Add sugar, 2 tablespoons at a time, and beat until the whites cling to the beaters solidly.

In another small bowl beat the egg yolks for about 1 minute, then add vanilla. Mix 1 large tablespoon of the whites into the yolks, then pour the mixture over remaining egg whites. Fold together, add ½ cup flour, 2 tablespoons at a time. Pour batter into jelly roll pan and spread evenly. Bake in middle of oven about 12 minutes or until cake draws slightly away from sides of pan, and a small knife inserted in the center comes out dry and clean.

Turn the cake out on a sheet of wax paper. Gently peel off top layer of paper. Let cake cool then cut in half, crosswise. Spread 1 layer with cup of marmalade or apricot preserves. If too thick to spread, thin by beating into it 1 or 2 tablespoons of orange juice. Place second layer on top. Mold softened ice cream on a sheet of aluminum foil into a brick, the length and width of the cake. Wrap in foil and freeze until solid.

MERINGUE:

8 egg whites
at room temperature
Pinch of salt
¾ cup super fine sugar

About 10 minutes before serving make the meringue. First, preheat broiler to its highest point. Then beat egg whites in salt until they form soft peaks. Still beating, slowly pour in the sugar and continue to beat for about 5 minutes or until egg whites are stiff and glossy.

Place cake on oven-proof baking dish. Remove ice cream from freezer and place on top of cake. Mash cake and ice cream on all sides with the meringue, shaping the top as decoratively as you like. Slide cake under broiler for 2 to 3 minutes and watch it carefully—it burns easily! Meringue should turn a pale golden brown in 2 to 3 minutes. Serve at once before ice cream begins to melt. (Serves 8)

MERINGUE SHELLS

6 eggs whites
½ teaspoon
cream of tartar
¼ teaspoon salt
1½ cups sugar

Beat egg whites until foamy. Add cream of tartar and salt; beat until stiff but not dry. Add sugar gradually beating until very stiff. Cover baking sheet with heavy brown paper. Pile meringue into 12 mounds about 3 inches in diameter. Make 2-inch depression in center. A pastry tube may be used to form meringues.

Bake in very slow oven, 275 degrees, for 1 hour. Meringues may be frozen until ready to use. For dessert, fill with ice cream, custard or fruit. (Yield: 12 meringue shells).

SUGARED PECANS

2 cups pecans
1 cup sugar
½ cup water
1 orange rind (grated)
and juice
1 teaspoon pure
vanilla flavoring

Boil water and sugar until a thin syrup forms. Flavor with orange rind and vanilla. Mix pecans into syrup and pour on greased surface. Break into pieces while warm.

BROWNIES

4 squares unsweetened chocolate
½ pound (2 sticks) butter or oleo
4 eggs
2 cups sugar
1 teaspoon vanilla
1 cup sifted flour
¼ teaspoon salt
2 cups chopped pecans

Melt chocolate with butter or oleo in a small saucepan. Beat eggs well in large mixer bowl. Gradually beat in sugar until mixture is fluffy-thick. (This takes about 10 minutes in an electric mixer.) Stir in vanilla and chocolate mixture,then fold in flour, salt and nuts until blended. Pour into two 8- x 8-inch baking pans and bake in 350-degree oven 25 minutes, or until shiny and firm on top. Do not overbake, middle should be fudge-like. Cool and cut into squares.

DATE CAKE

1 cup pitted chopped dates
1 cup walnuts or pecans
1½ cups sugar
1 cup salad oil
3 eggs
2 cups sifted flour
1 teaspoon baking soda
1 teaspoon salt
1 teaspoon nutmeg
1 teaspoon cinnamon
1 teaspoon allspice
1 cup buttermilk
1 teaspoon vanilla extract

Combine sugar, oil and egg; beat until smooth and creamy. Sift together dry ingredients; add alternately with buttermilk to creamed mixture. Mix until smooth. Stir in nuts, dates and vanilla.

Turn batter into a greased and floured 9- x 13- x 2-inch pan. Bake at 300 degrees for 55 to 60 minutes. Cool cake in pan. Spread with icing and cut into squares.

BUTTERMILK ICING

1 cup sugar
½ cup buttermilk
⅓ teaspoon baking soda
⅓ teaspoon vanilla extract
½ cup butter or oleo

Combine ingredients in saucepan. Cook over medium heat, stirring constantly, to softball stage. Remove from heat and cool 5 minutes. Beat mixture until it starts to thicken. Pour at once over cake in pan. (Yields about 1½ cups of icing)

YANKEE-REBEL FEUD CAKE

8 whole eggs
5 cups finely chopped pecans
2 cups granulated sugar
1 cup plain flour
1 teaspoon salt
4 teaspoons baking powder
1 tablespoon vanilla

Beat eggs at high speed for 5 minutes. Add sugar, vanilla, flour and baking powder and beat another 5 minutes. Add 5 cups pecans. Beat at low speed for one minute to moisten well. Pour into 3 greased and paper-lined 9-inch cake pans. Bake at 350 degrees about 15 to 20 minutes. Remove immediatley from pans to wire cake racks and cool. Cake may fall slightly but this is natural.

TOPPING:

1½ quarts whipping cream or dessert topping
¼ cup chopped pecans
1 cup powdered sugar (if whipping cream used)

Whip powdered sugar and cream until stiff. Frost layers, top and sides of cake and sprinkle generously with pecans.

P.S. The Rebs won!

APPLE CAKE ST. AMAND

4 cup apples, diced, peeled
2 cups sugar
2 eggs
2½ cups flour
1 cup pecans
2 teaspoons baking soda
1 teaspoon salt
1 teaspoon cinnamon
1 cup cooking oil

Mix apples and sugar; let stand ½ hour. Separate eggs. Beat yolks; beat whites until stiff. Fold yolks into whites. Fold in oil and let mixture set while you mix the dry ingredients.

Pour egg mixture over apples and stir in dry ingredients. Add nuts. Bake in greased tube pan at 350 degrees. Pears can be used instead of apples if desired. Bake 1 hour.

"SOCK IT TO ME" CAKE

1 box yellow cake mix, butter flavored
4 eggs
¾ cup Wesson Oil
1 cup chopped pecans
½ pint sour cream
1 stick butter
2 tablespoons sugar
1 tablespoon powdered cinnamon

In a large mixing bowl blend together the cake mix, oil and butter. Beat in eggs one at a time and beat according to directions on cake mix box. Fold in sour cream and pecans. Pour half the batter into a tube pan. Sprinkle sugar and cinnamon over batter in the pan, then cover with rest of batter. Do not stir.

Bake at 350 degrees for one hour. Test with a toothpick before removing from oven. Cool in pan for 5 minutes and turn onto cake platter.

MILK GLAZE:

1 cup powdered sugar
1 teaspoon vanilla flavor
2 tablespoons milk

Blend ingredients together. Drizzle over cake while cake is still warm. Your friends will want you to "sock it to them" several times.

AUNT HAPPY'S CAKE

2 sticks margarine
2½ cups sugar
5 eggs
1½ teaspoons coconut extract
1½ teaspoons rum extract
3 cups cake flour
1 teaspoon baking powder
1 cup homogenized milk

Beat margarine and sugar until light in color. Add eggs, one at a time, beating well before each egg is added. Add coconut and rum extracts. Mix flour and baking powder with milk and stir well together and combine all ingredients. Pour into angel cake loaf pan. Start in a cold oven. Set at 350 degrees and bake about an hour. This makes two small Bundt cakes and one large loaf cake.

GLAZE FOR CAKE:

1 cup granulated sugar
½ cup water
1 teaspoon almond extract

Glaze with sugar and water mixture. Bring to boil and boil for 5 minutes. Add almond extract and pour over cake.

DATE BALLS

2 sticks oleo
1 pound chopped dates
1 can coconut
1 cup dark brown sugar
1 cup light brown sugar
4 cups Rice Krispies
2 cups chopped pecans

Cook oleo, dates, coconut and sugar over low heat. Let come to a bubble and cook 6 minutes. Add 4 cups Rice Krispies and 2 cups chopped pecans. Make small balls and roll in powdered sugar.

WHISKEY BALLS

1 small package vanilla wafers, crushed
1 cup powdered sugar
4 jiggers whiskey
2 cups mixed nuts (pecans and walnuts), ground
3 tablespoons white Karo syrup

Stir in all ingredients together and shape into balls—about 1½-inch size.

BRANDY BALLS

3 small boxes vanilla wafers, crushed
1½ tablespoons cocoa
2 tablespoons white Karo syrup
1 cup powdered sugar
1 cup pecans, chopped
2½ jiggers brandy (about 8 tablespoons)

Mix all ingredients thoroughly and roll into balls. Sprinkle more powdered sugar on waxed paper and roll balls to coat. Store in closed container.

MOLASSES POPCORN BALLS

½ cup molasses
½ cup sugar
¼ teaspoon vinegar
¼ cup water
1¼ tablespoons butter
¼ teaspoon salt
6 cups popcorn, popped

Combine molasses, water, vinegar, sugar and salt. Cook slowly without stirring until small quantity dropped in water forms threads. Remove from heat, add butter and stir only enough to mix. Pour over popcorn, stirring constantly. Shape into balls and be quick about it.

NOTE: Molasses is inclined to cling to the cup or spoon or whatever you use to measure with. It will flow easily and will not cling if you grease the measure or rinse it in cold water.

LIZZIE'S COOKIES

1 cup brown sugar
1 stick margarine
4 eggs, beaten
3 teaspoons soda
3 tablespoons milk
3 cups flour
1 cup whiskey
1 teaspoon allspice
1 teaspoon cinnamon
1 teaspoon nutmeg
1 pound seeded raisins (about 3 cups)
1½ pounds pecans (6 cups), chopped
1 pound candied pineapple, small pieces
½ pound candied cherries, chopped
¼ pound dates, chopped

Cream butter and sugar; add well-beaten eggs. Sift flour and soda together; add to mixture a tablespoonful at a time. Add milk and half of whiskey. Add spices, rest of whiskey, fruit and mix well. Drop by teaspoonful on greased cookie sheet and bake in 275-degree oven for 20 to 30 minutes.

PARTY COOKIES

1 cup butter
2 eggs, separated
2 cups chopped pecans
½ cup brown sugar
2 cups sifted flour
Jelly

Cream butter, blend in brown sugar. Beat egg yolks until light, add to creamed mixture, blending well. Blend in flour. Chill dough 2 hours.

Beat egg whites until frothy. Shape chilled dough into walnut-size balls, dip into beaten egg whites, then roll in chopped pecans. Place on greased baking sheet and make a depression in center of each. Bake in oven at 350 degrees for 8 minutes. Remove from oven and press down centers again. Continue baking 10 minutes more.

Cool slightly, fill centers with jelly. Makes about 48 cookies. Store in airtight container.

PEACH FLAMBEAU

1 can peach halves
2 cloves for each half
Cinnamon
1 ounce brandy for each half

Set peach halves in a shallow baking pan. Stick 2 cloves in center of each and sprinkle with peach juice and pour balance in pan. Pour in 1 ounce brandy for each peach half. Bake in 450-degree oven until rim browns. Remove and ignite immediately.

BANANA NUT BREAD

1 stick margarine
1 cup sugar
2 large ripe bananas, well mashed
1 tablespoon soda
2 tablespoons boiling water
2 eggs, slightly beaten
1 teaspoon lemon juice
½ cup chopped nuts
2 cups sifted flour

Cream sugar and margarine until light and fluffy; add bananas. Place soda in hot water. Add dissolved soda, eggs, lemon juice, nuts and flour to creamed mixture. Sitr just enough to combine ingredients. Pour batter into wax paper-lined loaf pan. Bake at 350 degrees for 1 hour. Remove bread from pan and peel off paper. Serve warm or cold.

CREOLE STYLE HOMEMADE PEACH ICE CREAM

½-gallon or gallon-size ice cream freezer
3 cups light cream
2 cups sliced, sweetened peaches
¾ cup sugar
¼ teaspoon almond extract
¼ teaspoon salt
2 egg yolks
1 cup milk
1 tablespoon flour

In a double boiler combine sugar, flour and salt. In a small bowl beat egg yolks slightly; add milk and mix well. Stir into sugar mixture. Cook over hot water, stirring constantly, until thickened. Pour in large bowl to cool and add cream, peaches and extract.

Place dasher in freezer can; add ice cream mixture. Cover, adjust crank, and pack 8 parts ice to 1 part freezer salt around can. Turn dasher slowly until ice partially melts and forms a brine. After 5 to 10 minutes increase speed and turn constantly until turning becomes difficult.

Remove ice from around top of can, take off lid and remove dasher. Plug opening in lid and replace lid. Drain off brine. Pack 4 parts ice to 1 part salt around freezer can. Cover and let stand 3 or 4 hours to ripen. (Makes 1⅓ quarts)

TONY'S CREOLE CUSTARD FLAN

1 cup cream
1 cup milk
1 teaspoon vanilla flavoring
3 eggs
2 egg yolks
1 cup sugar
¼ cup water
6 teaspoons crushed almonds

Scald cream and milk in pot; add vanilla. Combine the eggs, egg yolks and ½ cup sugar and beat until well blended. Gradually pour milk into egg mixture stirring constantly.

In a heavy skillet heat remaining sugar over moderate heat (350 degrees) until it is melted. Gradually add water and boil until well blended and brown. Pour this caramel equally into 6 custard cups. Sprinkle 1 teaspoon crushed almonds into each cup. When it sets pour custard into cups and place them in a pan of hot water. Bake in moderate oven 45 minutes or until knife inserted in center comes out clean.

Cool. When cold unmold onto serving dishes. You may use tube pan or single mold, if desired. You may serve with whipped cream. (Serves 6)

CREOLE PECAN CUSTARD

¾ cups chopped pecans
6 eggs
2 cups milk
2 cups sugar
4 tablespoons flour
1 tablespoon butter

First, mix the flour with 1 cup sugar, then cream the butter with the second cup of sugar; add the well-beaten yolks of eggs, the beaten white, flour and sugar, milk, and lastly, the nuts. Mix all well together, pour into a well buttered baking dish and bake in a moderate oven. Custard may be served hot or cold with whipped cream.

PATSY'S BLACKBERRY COBBLER

CRUST:

1½ cups Bisquick flour
2 tablespoons sugar
½ cup milk

FILLING:

2 pints fresh blackberries (cooked, sweetened and thickened)
¼ stick butter
2 tablespoons sugar

Mix together first 3 ingredients. Roll out ⅔ for bottom crust, saving remaining ⅓. Fit into 1-quart Pyrex loaf pan. Pour in blackberries, dot with butter. Roll out remaining ⅓ Bisquick mix and fit on top of berries. Bring sides of bottom crust over and seal. Sprinkle with sugar. Bake at 400 degrees for 30 to 40 minutes or until golden brown. You may substitute any fresh fruit. (Serves 6)

TONY'S CREPE SUZETTES

1 cup flour
2 tablespoons powdered sugar
1 cup milk
2 eggs
1 tablespoon melted butter

Sift flour twice, then add milk and eggs. Use rotary beater until smooth. Add melted butter. Make into small thin pancakes on a well buttered medium hot skillet.

SAUCE:

1 cup sugar
½ cup butter
Juice and grated rind of two oranges
Tablespoon lemon juice
Tablespoon sherry

Stir sugar and butter until light and soft, then add other ingredients. Heat sauce and pour over pancakes. You may try a teaspoon strawberry preserves, cherries or other fruit on each pancake and roll with toothpick.

LOUISIANA RICE PUDDING

4 cups milk
½ cup molasses
½ cup washed rice
½ teaspoon cinnamon
½ teaspoon salt
½ cup raisins
1 tablespoon butter

Mix well all ingredients except butter. Bake in slow oven, 275 to 300 degrees, for 2½ hours, stirring every 15 minutes for first hour. Add butter at fourth stirring. (Serves 6)

KIDDY PEANUT BUTTER CANDY WHEELS

White of large egg
12-ounce jar peanut butter
1 pound powdered sugar

Whip egg white until stiff, adding powdered sugar slowly until smooth and the consistency of dough.
Divide in 2 squares ¼-inch thick. Cover evenly with peanut butter. Roll into loaves, wrap in wax paper and refrigerate overnight. Cut into ½-inch wheels. Kids love it and it's easy to make.

HOLIDAY TREAT

1 quart milk
6 eggs, separated
6 tablespoons sugar
3 envelopes of gelatin
⅓ cup water
2 cups chopped pecans
1 medium package vanilla wafers
½ pint whipping cream, whipped
Vanilla or sherry to taste

Heat milk slowly. Beat egg whites and yolks separately. Add 6 heaping tablespoons sugar to egg yolks. Stir yolks slowly into milk and cook until custard has thickened. Soak gelatin in cold water and stir into milk and eggs. Cool slightly then stir in whipped whites. Flavor with vanilla or sherry.
Into a large oblong dish pour a cup of the pudding, then a layer of pecans followed by wafers. Continue until all ingredients are used. Place in refrigerator until firm. Serve with whipped cream. (Serves 12)

LES OREILLES de COCHON

½ cup melted butter
2 eggs
½ teaspoon salt
2 cups sifted flour

Beat eggs slightly, add melted butter. Add flour and salt and stir until well blended. Pinch off a small ball of dough and roll out very thinly. Roll dough into cone shape pinching bottom together so that other end resembles a pig's ear.
Heat oil in large skillet or in deep-fryer to high heat. Reduce to medium heat. Fry 2 or 3 ears at a time until brown. Drain on paper toweling. Cool.

TOPPING FOR PIG'S EARS

1 cup pure cane syrup
½ cup chopped nut meals

Pour syrup into large saucepan (it likes to boil up and bubble) and cook to the soft ball stage. Remove toweling from ears and pour the hot syrup over them until coated. Sprinkle chopped nuts over ears before syrup dries.

BREAD PUDDING with WHISKEY SAUCE

2 cups milk
4 cups coarse bread crumbs
¼ cup melted butter
½ cup sugar
2 eggs, slightly beaten
¼ teaspoon salt
½ cup seedless raisins
1 teaspoon cinnamon

Scald milk and pour over bread crumbs. Cool and add remaining ingredients, mixing well. Pour into a 1½ quart casserole. Place casserole in pan of hot water (1 inch deep) and bake at 350 degrees for 1 hour, or until a silver knife inserted into pudding comes out clean.

WHISKEY SAUCE

1 stick butter or margarine
1 egg
1 cup sugar
¼ cup whiskey

Cook butter and sugar together in double boiler until mixture is very hot, thick and sugar dissolved. Add egg quickly and beat. Cool slightly and add whiskey. Serve hot or cold over pudding.

TONY'S CAJUN COUNTRY COOKBOOK

I was tickled, pleased, delighted, when through the mail there came,
Tony's Cajun Country Cookbook, my day was not the same.

I sat right down to look it through, page by page by page,
so many luscious recipes, my kitchen was my stage.

When I read of one good recipe, I cried upon my pillow,
cuz up here in the north by us, we've no tasty armadillo!

But we do have coon a-plenty, and 'possums by the score,
just once I erred and caught a skunk, I don't do that anymore!

Our favorite recipe thus far, among the cajun treats,
is your tasty, tasty boudin, made of spicy creole meats.

With parsley and some peppers, and onions by the score,
with rice and cloves of garlic, ah, we couldn't ask for more.

Before we left your lovely state, better cookin' was our reasoning
I bought a big 'ole can of that Tony's Famous Creole Seasoning.

I figured if we took it back, I'd experiment and cook,
I'd no idea right at that time, Tony'd written quite a book.

With how to fix so many things, to give the buds a treat,
in the very truest cajun style, when tongue and palate meet.

We now know why he said it, we'll know it till we die,
why Tony coined his famous phrase, "Tonight, I'll make 'em cry!"

by Carole Magnus
Fredericktown, Missouri

BEVERAGES
HORS D'OEUVRES
DELICACIES

RUSSELL GREEN'S ROLLED ALLIGATOR ROAST

Slice a skinned alligator tail from one end to the other just like you fillet a fish. This will give you a fillet about 3 feet long, 1 inch thick and 6 inches wide. Season generously with Tony Chachere's Famous Creole Seasoning and sprinkle all over with a mixture of onions, bell pepper, and garlic all chopped fine. Roll the fillet and tie with string in about 4 places to hold in place. Melt one stick Oleo in Dutch oven. Place roast in oven and cover with slices of bacon. Heat oven to 500 degrees and cook until bacon is crisp. Then pour one cup white wine over roast and set oven to 300 degrees. Cover and let cook until tender about 2 hours.

To me this is the finest way of all to cook alligator. (Serves 8.) (But if you are a Robichaux, serves only 2.) Russell Green of Kaplan, Louisiana is a prominent Brahma cattle breeder and outstanding sportsman. Thank you Russell, for this outstanding recipe.

LAGNIAPPE

GARBO'S CAPONATA

3 tablespoons sugar
1 small jar sliced green olives with pimento
1 small bottle capers with liquid
¼ cup olive oil
Salt and pepper to taste
1 eggplant, diced
1 stick celery, chopped
1 medium bell pepper, chopped
1 onion, chopped
2 cloves garlic, minced
½ small can tomato paste
¾ cup water

Soak diced eggplant in salt water about ½ hour. Drain water. Saute onion, celery, garlic and bell pepper in olive oil until soft. Add tomato paste, cook well. Add water, sugar, salt and pepper and cook until thick. Add olives, capers and eggplant. Simmer 10 minutes. Remove from heat and let cool to room temperature.

Serve as appetizer with crackers.

CREOLE DRIPPED COFFEE

To make good Creole coffee use a drip coffee pot (or a Drip-o-Lator), dark roast coffee (ground rather than fine) and fresh boiling water. Scald pot and dripper. Allow 2 heaping tablespoons grounds for every cup coffee. Pour about 10 tablespoons boiling water in pot, wait until grounds settle and stop bubbling. Every 2 or 3 minutes pour about 2 tablespoons boiling water over the grounds until desired quantity is made.

Scald demi-tasse (small) cups to heat them (if preferred) and immediately pour the hot, dark black coffee and serve.

IRISH COFFEE

Dark roast coffee
1 jigger Irish whiskey
2 teaspoons sugar
Whipped cream, sweetened

Drip coffee in drip-o-lator or drip coffee pot. To one cup coffee add whiskey, sugar and top with cream.

CAFE DIABLE

2 cups black coffee
8 lumps sugar
2 cups warm cognac
4 cloves
Rind of ½ lemon
Rind of ½ orange

Preheat a silver bowl and ladle with hot water. Into the bowl pour in the cognac and add six lumps of sugar, the cloves and the lemon and orange rind. Dip up a ladle of brandy, place two more lumps of sugar in it and set cognac afire. Lower flaming ladle into the bowl and very slowly pour in the coffee, stirring constantly, while dipping ladles of coffee-brandy mixture and pouring it back until all brandy is ablaze. When the flame dies serve the Cafe Diable in demi-tasse cups.

WILD CHERRY BOUNCE

1 quart wild cherries
1 pound sugar
1 fifth bourbon

Wash and pick over cherries, removing stems, and drain. Pour moist cherries into a half-gallon jug. Pour ½ cup sugar over moist cherries, then shake until cherries are coated. Pour remaining sugar on top of cherries. Do not mix. Place cap on jug loosely to prevent pressure build-up. Let stand until sugar melts on top of cherries, then stir by revolving jug. Repeat until all sugar is dissolved.

Let stand for 2 months. Pour bourbon over cherries and close jug tightly. Let stand 3 or 4 months. During the 3 month period, revolve jug occasionally. Strain through cheesecloth and pour into bottles. (Makes about ½ gallon)

BLACKBERRY WINE

4 quarts blackberries
3½ pounds brown sugar
Boiling water to cover

Cover blackberries with boiling water and let stand for 2 hours. Then squeeze through a cheesecloth and add sugar to the liquid. Pour liquid in an open jar, cover with cheesecloth, and let stand until fermenting ceases. Then bottle. Simple!

CREOLE EGG NOG

12 eggs
2 cups sugar
1 cup bourbon whiskey
1 quart whipping cream
2 teaspoons grated nutmeg

Whip cream until stiff, adding ½ cup sugar, 1 tablespoon at a time. Break eggs and separate. Beat egg yolks, slowly adding 1 cup sugar. Beat until sugar is dissolved and the mixture smooth. Whip egg whites to frothy peaks by addition of ½ cup sugar, 1 tablespoon at a time. Mix yolks with bourbon, add whipped cream. Fold in egg whites, sprinkle with nutmeg and serve.

BULL SHOT

2 parts vodka
2 parts beef bouillon
Dash lemon juice
Dash Tabasco sauce
Dash Worcestershire sauce
Pinch of salt and pepper

Stir ingredients with a spoon and pour into glass filled with ice cubes. Takes the place of a Bloody Mary.

SAZERAC COCKTAIL

3 dashes absinthe (substitute anisette or herbsaint)
1 jigger bourbon or rye
1 lump sugar
1 dash orange bitters
1 dash Angostura bitters
Twist of lemon

Place ingredients in cocktail shaker. Shake well and pour into Old Fashion glass with plenty of cracked ice. Add a twist of lemon and serve.

RAMOS GIN FIZZ

Ice (about 1 cup)
1 egg white
2 teaspoons thick cream
1 heaping teaspoon sugar
Juice of ½ lemon
2 ounces gin
½ teaspoon orange flower water
1 dash Pechaud bitters

Put above ingredients in blender and blend until frosty (almost like whipped cream), then serve.

CREAM de MENTHE FRAPPE

1 quart vanilla ice cream
¼ cup brandy
1 cup green Cream de Menthe

Soften ice cream and beat all ingredients in a mixer. Place in ice trays and let stand 10 hours. Serve in champagne glasses. (Serves 6)

GOLDEN CHAMPAGNE PUNCH

6-ounce can frozen orange juice concentrate
1 cup lemon juice
1 No. 2 can pineapple juice
1 cup sugar
4/5 quart sauterne wine
4/5 quart champagne

Mix the fruit juices and sugar, stir to dissolve sugar; cover, chill in refrigerator several hours. Just before serving pour mixture over ice block in a punch bowl. Add chilled sauterne and champagne. Serve at once. Garnish with orange slices, maraschino cherries or strawberries as desired. (Makes about 5½ quarts)

BRANDY FRUIT CHAMPAGNE

Use a glass bowl and assemble frozen strawberries, bits of peaches, cherries and pineapple chunks. Cover with brandy to marinate and chill in refrigerator for 1 hour or a whole day. Place a few pieces of each of the brandied-fruit in a champagne glass, cover with champagne and serve.

JALAPENO PEPPER
Hors d'Oeuvre

1 dozen green pickled jalapeno peppers
1 small can potted meat
2 tablespoons chopped sweet pickles
2 tablespoons mayonnaise
½ dozen salted crackers (crumbled)

Mix potted meat, pickles, mayonnaise and enough cracker crumbs to make a thick, moist paste.

Cut the tip-end off peppers, remove seeds and membrane. Fill peppers with above mixture. Serve as hors d'oeuvre.

After a few drinks they are not so fiery.

HOT PEPPER JELLY

¾ cup sweet bell peppers, ground
¼ cup Louisiana hot peppers, ground, red or green, preferably both
5½ cups sugar
1½ cups apple cider vinegar
1 small bottle of Certo

Remove seeds and grind peppers in food chopper. Save juice and mix with vinegar and sugar. Bring to a full boil, about 5 minutes. Add ground peppers, cook 2 minutes. Cool for 5 minutes, then add Certo. Bring to a full rolling boil for about 1 or 2 minutes, then cool about 5 minutes. Skim and pour into glasses and seal with paraffin. IMPORTANT: Wear rubber gloves or plastic ones when handling hot peppers and watch out for your eyes.

PINK PICKLED EGGS

6 eggs
1 cup canned beet juice
1 cup cider vinegar
1 garlic clove, crushed
½ bay leaf
¼ teaspoon ground allspice
1 teaspoon salt
Freshly ground black pepper

Hard boil eggs. Plunge into cold water and shell immediately. Put eggs in a quart jar. Combine remaining ingredients, bring to a boil and pour over eggs. Cover, cool and refrigerate overnight or for at least 8 hours.

BIG ALABAMA BAYOU ROASTED PECANS & HOT BUTTERED RUM

Melt butter in a frying pan. Add pecans, sprinkled with a little salt, and fry until slightly brown. Delicious with hot, buttered rum . . . while sitting in a rocking chair . . . in front of a roaring fire . . . raindrops falling on the roof.

HOT BUTTERED RUM

1 pat butter
1 jigger rum
1 teaspoon sugar
1 teaspoon lemon juice
Dash powdered cinnamon
1 cup boiling hot water

Place butter in a mug. Add rum, sugar and lemon juice. Pour in the hot water and sprinkle with cinnamon.

SHRIMP CANAPES

1 pint fresh homemade mayonnaise
½ pound Cheddar cheese, grated
3 dozen Ritz crackers
3 dozen medium shrimp, boiled and seasoned
3 dozen slices dill pickles

When ready to serve place crackers on cookie sheet with round of pickle on top. Place shrimp on top of pickle. Make a sauce mixture of mayonnaise and chese and place portion on top of shrimp. Cook in 425-degree oven until sauce bubbles. (Makes 36)

CRACKERS DELUXE

For Salads, Cocktails and Soups

Dip crackers, one side only, in melted butter, sprinkle generously with paprika and place in a broiler until brown.

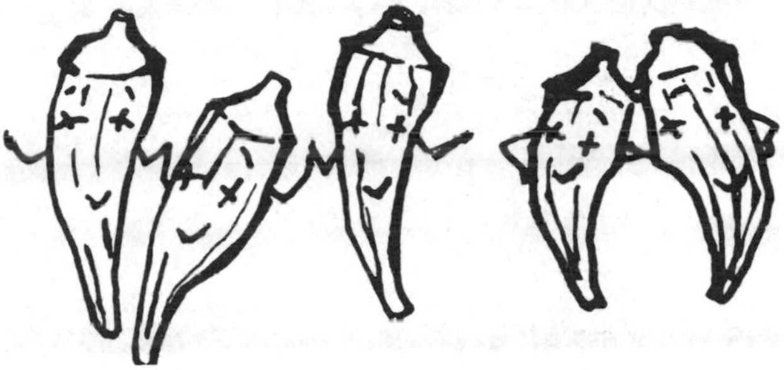

PICKLED OKRA

4 pounds small tender okra
¾ cup plain salt
8 cups white vinegar
1 cup water
10 cloves garlic
10 pods red or green peppers, (Louisiana Red Hots)
Celery salt or mustard seed (optional)

Wash and sterilize 10 pint jars. Wash okra and leave stems on. Pack in jar, stems up. Place 1 pepper pod and 1 garlic clove in each hot jar. Bring vinegar, water and salt to a boil, remove from fire immediately. Add 1 teaspoon celery salt or mustard seed if desired. Pour boiling-hot mixture over okra and seal jar. Let stand 2 months before using.

TOMATO PICKLES

1 gallon quartered green tomatoes
1 quart white cut onions, rings or quarters
½ pint green hot peppers or red and green for coloring (You may use less, according to taste)
1½ quarts distilled vinegar
3 cups sugar
½ cup salt
1 tablespoon black pepper

Heat all ingredients just before boiling point. Fill hot jars and seal. Set aside 2 weeks before using.

SHRIMP HORS D'OEUVRES

Marinate drained canned shrimp in French dressing for about 1 hour. Serve individually, on cocktail toothpicks.

Roll each whole canned shrimp (jelly-roll fashion) in one-half sliced bacon. Skewer with toothpicks. Broil until bacon is crisp and brown. Serve hot.

Spread thin slices of cucumber (or cucumber pickle) with mayonnaise. Lay a shrimp on each slice. Serve on thin rounds of lightly toasted bread.

Split large-size canned shrimp lengthwise. Insert small portions of Roquefort cheese. Roll shrimp in flour, then in one beaten egg, mixed with one tablespoon water. Saute to light brown in hot fat in a skillet. Serve on toothpicks, or on thin rounds of toast.

CREAMY NUTTY TUNA SANDWICHES

8-ounce package Philadelphia Cream Cheese
2 tablespoons lemon juice
½ cup mayonnaise
1 cup flaked tuna
½ cup ripe olives, chopped
Butter
Bread

Blend together cream cheese, lemon juice and mayonnaise. Fold in chopped olives and flaked tuna. Season. Spread all slices of bread with butter, then with filling. Remove crust from sandwiches, and cut in triangles. Butter edges and dip in chopped pecans. Garnish with sweet pickle sticks and potato chips. Place in freezer until needed.

HAM BALLS

Combine:

2 cups ground ham (lean)
3 hard-boiled egg yolks
1 tablespoon onion puree
½ teaspoon Tabasco
¼ cup Parmesan cheese
½ teaspoon Tony's Famous Creole Seasoning

Roll ham mixture into bite size balls, dip in melted butter, then roll each one in finely chopped almonds. Chill thoroughly before serving.

SWEDISH MEAT BALLS

6 pounds ground meat (beef with approximately ¼ pork)
6 slices stale bread, soaked in milk
3 whole eggs, beaten
Garlic salt
Salt and black pepper
½ cup parsley, chopped fine
½ cup green onion tops, chopped fine
2 medium white onions, chopped fine
4 sticks celery, chopped fine

SAUCE:

2 large jars barbecue sauce
2 cans mushroom soup

My barbecue sauce will be fantastic. Order from back of book.

Mix ingredients and roll into bite-size balls. Fry in small amount of fat. Pour off excess fat and mix barbecue sauce and mushroom soup in remaining drippings. Pour over meatballs which have been placed in a large saucepan and simmer 40 to 45 minutes. (Makes between 400 and 450 meatballs.)

VEAL SCALLOPINI DIP

6 to 8 pounds U.S. Choice veal
Paper bag
Flour
Oil for frying
Oregano
Water
Tony's Famous Creole Seasoning

Thinly slice veal into small pieces, 1 x 2 inches. Place flour, seasoned with Tony's Famous Creole Seasoning, in paper bag. Dredge meat. Fry in deep fat until brown. Drain fat from pan, leaving drippings. Put meat back in pan and season with oregano to taste. Add a small amount of water, cover and simmer until meat is coated with thick gravy. Serve in chafing dish. Arrange cocktail picks around dish to eat with. Delicious! Serves a large crowd.

CUCUMBER-CHICKEN SPREAD

1 cup canned chicken, chopped fine
½ cup finely chopped cucumber
Mayonnaise (preferably homemade)
½ teaspoon Tabasco
½ teaspoon Tony's Famous Creole Seasoning or salt and pepper to taste

Combine chopped chicken and cucumbers and blend with mayonnaise and other ingredients. Mix well, chill and spread on crackers.

DEVILED HAM DIP

1 jar pimento cheese spread
½ cup mayonnaise
2 tablespoons deviled ham
1 teaspoon grated onions

Have all ingredients at room temperature. Blend together in electric mixer or with a fork. Serve with potato chips or flowerettes of cauliflower.

STUFFED CELERY

Cut celery into pieces convenient for handling. Fill the hollows with soft cheese, plain or mixed with chopped pimento, green peppers, nuts, olives or a combination of two or more of these. Serve on a plate with another salad or as a relish.

Send me __________ copies of the Microwave Cajun Country Cookbook at the regular price $8.95 plus $1.00 for postage & handling.

Enclosed is my check or money order for $__________

Name ______________________________

Street ______________________________

City ______________ State __________ Zip __________

Make payable to:

CREOLE FOODS OF OPELOUSAS, INC.
P.O. Box 1687 Opelousas, LA 70571

Send Me __________ copies of the La. Original Creole Seafood Recipes at the regular price $8.95 plus $1.00 for postage & handling.

Enclosed is my check or money order for $__________

Name ______________________________

Street ______________________________

City ______________ State __________ Zip __________

Make payable to:

CREOLE FOODS OF OPELOUSAS, INC.
P.O. Box 1687 Opelousas, LA 70571

Send me ______________ case(s) of Tony's Creole Crab Boil 9 oz. size (12 to case) at $16.50 per case shipped prepaid. (Sorry, no broken cases.) Case contains one dozen 9 oz. sifter top cartons.

Enclosed is my check or money order for $__________

Name ______________________________

Street ______________________________

City ______________ State __________ Zip __________

Make payable to:

CREOLE FOODS OF OPELOUSAS, INC.
P.O. Box 1687 Opelousas, LA 70571

Send me ______________ case(s)of Tony's Creole Barbecue Sauce 18 oz. size (12 to case) at $30.00 per case shipped prepaid. (Sorry, no broken cases.) Case contains one dozen 18 oz. bottles.

Enclosed is my check or money order for $__________

Name ______________________________

Street ______________________________

City ______________ State __________ Zip __________

Make payable to:

CREOLE FOODS OF OPELOUSAS, INC.
P.O. Box 1687 Opelousas, LA 70571

TONY CHACHERE'S

"Creole Hot Sauce"

A Flavor that is "So Exciting" and "So Unusual" That it enhances anything it is put on!

A perfect blend of Cayenne Peppers, Crushed Garlic, Chopped Onions, Tomatoes, Vinegar and Spices.

GREAT ON

Hamburgers, Meat Loaf, Fish,Fried Chicken, Pizza, Eggs and all Seafood.

ADD TO

Soups, Stews and Sauces.

OR

Use as a dip with chips.

Try the Following:

Add one teaspoon to each four eggs before scrambling.

-or-

Place one 8 ounce square of Velveeta Processed Cheese on plate, cover with Hot Sauce and use as a dip with chips or crackers.

-or-

For a fantastic Salad Dressing, mix one tablespoon Hot Sauce to four tablespoons Mayonnaise.

Packed 12/6-oz. Bottles to Case.

Send me ________________ copies of the New Revised Cookbook at the regular price $8.95 plus $1.00 for postage and handling.

Enclosed is my check or money order for $ ________.

Name ________________________________

Street ________________________________

City ________________ State ________________ Zip ______

Make payable to:

CREOLE FOODS OF OPELOUSAS, INC.
P.O. Box 1687 Opelousas, LA 70571

Send me ________________ case(s) of Tony's Instant Creole Roux and Gravy Mix at $21.00 per case shipped prepaid. (Sorry, no broken cases.) Case contains one dozen 10 oz. sifter top cartons.

Enclosed is my check or money order for $______.

Name ________________________________

Street ________________________________

City ________________ State ________________ Zip ______

Make payable to:

CREOLE FOODS OF OPELOUSAS, INC.
P.O. Box 1687 Opelousas, LA 70571

Send me ________________ case(s)of Tony's Famous Creole Seasoning 8 oz. size (12 to case) at $18.15 per case shipped prepaid. (Sorry, no broken cases.) Case contains one dozen 8 oz. sifter top cartons.

Enclosed is my check or money order for $______.

Name ________________________________

Street ________________________________

City ________________ State ________________ Zip ______

Make payable to:

CREOLE FOODS OF OPELOUSAS, INC.
P.O. Box 1687 Opelousas, LA 70571

Send me ________________ case(s) of Tony Chachere's Creole Seafood Sauce at $24.00 per case shipped prepaid. (Sorry, no broken cases.)

Enclosed is my check or money order for $______.

Name ________________________________

Street ________________________________

City ________________ State ________________ Zip ______

Make payable to:

CREOLE FOODS OF OPELOUSAS, INC.
P.O. Box 1687 Opelousas, LA 70571

Send me ________________ case(s)of Tony's Famous Creole Seasoning 17 18 oz. size (12 to case) at $30.50 per case shipped prepaid. (Sorry, no broken cases.) Case contains one dozen 17 oz. sifter top cartons.

Enclosed is my check or money order for $________.

Name ________________________________

Street ________________________________

City ________________ State ________________ Zip ________________

Make payable to:

CREOLE FOODS OF OPELOUSAS, INC.
P.O. Box 1687 Opelousas, LA 70571